GW00363260

MY OTHER WORLD

MY OTHER WORLD

MARGARET WHITLAM

ALLEN&UNWIN

This paperback edition published in 2002

First published in 2001

Allen & Unwin
83 Alexander Street
Crows Nest, NSW 2065
Australia
Phone: (61 2) 8425 0100
Fax: (61 2) 9906 2218
Email: info@allenandunwin.com
Web: www.allenandunwin.com

National Library of Australia
Cataloguing-in-Publication entry:

Whitlam, Margaret, 1919– .
  Margaret Whitlam: my other world.

  ISBN 1 86508 781 5 (pbk)

  1. Whitlam, Margaret, 1920—Journeys. 2. Whitlam,
  Margaret, 1920—Journeys—Europe. 3. Women travellers—
  Biography. I. Title. II. Title: My other world.

910.92

Set in 10.5 pt Life by Midland Typesetters, Maryborough
Printed by Griffin Press, South Australia
Text design by Liz Seymour

10 9 8 7 6 5 4 3 2 1

CONTENTS

To my dear husband, who still says
he taught me everything I know

Acknowledgments

MY THANKS GO TO the people who really made this book possible—travellers from Australia and helpers in many countries. I hope the result conveys some of the pleasures we had together.

Over the years I have collected a great number of photographs of our travels. Some of those reproduced here I have taken myself, but most have been given to me. I particularly want to thank Dr Jo Woolmington for the photo that was used on the cover of this book and Norm Keogh who is the photographer responsible for reminders of the epic journeys across Russia and through South America. I thank everyone who has given me precious memories—and has given the reader some light and colour.

For ten years John Wellings, Anne Krone and I worked as a very special team in planning and leading the study tours. We continued as a team as we recalled the experiences of those years. Without this help I would have achieved nothing. Thank you, best friends.

Margaret Whitlam

SETTING OFF

'NEVER MIND THE WHYS or wherefores' sings someone in a Gilbert and Sullivan operetta. Maybe that's right, for the whys and wherefores of this book are many.

Why did I write it? Well, people kept saying, 'You could write a book . . . you should write a book' as I added more and more countries and experiences to my travelling. So with more than a little help from my friends, here we are.

This is a story of my travels as the leader of group study tours around the world. It starts in 1990, when I had just entered my seventies, and continues for a decade. The planning and leading of tours were a major part of my life for these ten years, involving hundreds of people travelling with me and dozens of people assisting in many countries. I will introduce you to a few of those who travelled with me—and I hope you will be able to keep track of them throughout the book. I will also tell you about some of those who helped us in the countries we visited.

An important part of those tours was Anne Krone and John Wellings, whom I first got to know when we were involved in adult education. We were part of a team that organised the International Conference on Adult Education as part of Australia's bicentenary in 1988. In the years following that conference Anne and John told me of their ideas to organise overseas study tours. I knew the venture they were proposing would be both successful and enjoyable and leapt at the invitation to work with them again. We planned to organise tours on which our travellers could really learn something worthwhile in the countries we visited, so the name we chose—International Study Programs, often referred to simply as ISP—was very appropriate.

You will meet Anne and John throughout this book. Their backgrounds and experience—they had both worked extensively with UNESCO and on other international activities—complemented mine. We became a close-knit and successful team. Regularly the three of us would sit down with maps and a whiteboard to plan the program ahead. As we worked out the principles on which we would operate, we settled on offering mainly three-week tours for an average of thirty participants. We developed themes that ranged from literary tours of England to music tours of Central Europe. In the long run, we organised travels to study the history and culture of nearly thirty different countries.

Background notes were always sent out to participants before departure, and seminars and lectures by highly qualified speakers were held along the way. ISP planned an average of three nights at each stopover to allow time to appreciate each place and to make travel enjoyable. Most meals were included and were taken in surroundings typical of the region we were in. No one dined alone unless they wanted to and place cards at dinner made it possible for everyone to take turns sitting at the leader's table and, indeed, to get to know each other.

In this record, taken mostly from my diaries and journals, it's given me enormous pleasure to revisit the countries on the list of a decade. Perhaps it's naive to admit enjoying the tangible souvenirs of pleasant places, turning over the collection of theatre tickets, gallery tickets, room allocation cards, menus . . . The only thing better is looking through the album of selections of everyone's photos. This was presented to me at a dinner attended by more than one hundred of our travellers, celebrating my ten years of group travel. It surely showed that there is a special benefit—a camaraderie—that comes from such travel.

Although I started out as lone leader, I was joined, after a year or so and for many of the tours, by my life's partner, ostensibly retired! In total we were to lead eighteen 'Whitlam Tours', accompanied by John and Anne as managers. Here, in a small collection of memories of those journeys you'll find some of the places and some of the people appreciated by us all.

At the end of one fascinating day on our travels I noted in my diary: 'Sometimes I think we're in another world.' I invite you to join me as I take you to *My Other World*.

THE HEART OF FRANCE

SITTING HIGH IN A COACH was a different way for me to travel from Charles de Gaulle airport to downtown Paris. I had made the journey often before, but it had usually been in an Embassy car. This time I had thirty people who were depending on me to show them something of France. In the next three weeks we would not only explore Paris, but travel through the very heart of the country.

As we headed towards the city through the mists of the early morning I could make out the church of the Sacré Coeur de Montmartre and it seemed to be beckoning to us. People were starting to move around the streets and shops of their arrondissements—they are much more like separate villages than suburbs. There is *always* a sense of excitement for me in arriving in Paris. I could feel that excitement now, despite some apprehension about my new responsibilities in leading a group, but I certainly knew that I have a special love for France.

Our hotel, Jardin de Cluny, was located near the Musée Cluny on the left bank of the Seine, and as soon as I had settled in I slipped out to explore that neighbourhood. One of the delightful things about Paris is that wherever you are there is a shop nearby which sells baguettes and another for cheeses and other things needed for a snack or light lunch. The wines range from those that are cheaper than the bottled water to really fine regional selections. The shops are uniquely French, quite different to a corner store or deli in Australia, or even other parts of Europe. Part of their appeal is the rather jolly shopkeeper who usually speaks good English, but responds warmly to a 'Bonjour, Monsieur' or a 'Bonsoir, Madame.'

Betty was one of the participants on our first tour, and she is one of those you will meet again. She was such a pleasant person to have with us, always friendly and helpful and on for a bit of fun. For years she had owned a chocolate shop in Mosman, on Sydney's lower north shore, and she greeted people with a quite delicious smile. One of the nice things about people like Betty is that they appreciate arrangements made for them. After a few days in Paris Betty announced that she needed only two words of French. 'What are they?' I asked. ' "Magnifique" and "merci". I go into a shop and say "magnifique". Someone comes running over and asks what I would like. I say "merci" and I can get whatever I want.' Betty knew how to get on with people.

The afternoon we arrived we went on a coach tour of the city—always a delight for me. For many of the group it was their first time here and I looked forward to showing them my favourite places. We were soon crossing the Seine and stopping at that grandest of buildings, the Notre Dame de Paris with its twin bell towers, statues and flying buttresses. We drove on past the Louvre and into the Rue de Rivoli. As we passed the Tuileries Gardens I pointed out l'Orangerie where we would return later to see the Monet water lilies and other great art works. From the Place de la Concorde we travelled up the magnificent Champs Elysées to the Arc de Triomphe. Crossing back to the left bank we came to the Eiffel Tower, leading down to the Champs de Mars and the Ecole Militaire. Beyond is the headquarters of the United Nations Educational, Scientific and Cultural Organization (UNESCO), with which I was *very* familiar. Near the Eiffel Tower is the Australian Embassy, which had been home to Gough and me for nearly four years.

I had been invited to take the group to the Australian Embassy so that all could see the superb view of Paris from the rooftop. The embassy had been purpose-built in the 1970s to a Harry Seidler design, and we had lived there in the mid 1980s, when Gough had been Australia's Ambassador to UNESCO. In those days an invitation to our quarters was much sought after on evenings such as 14 July, when the fireworks were virtually in our front yard. During the daytime there is a great view across the Seine to the Palais de Chaillot, with its fountains and handsome bronze sculptures in front of the colonnaded buildings. I couldn't help feeling a little homesick for our old abode.

The big white church of Sacré Coeur looms large at the top of Montmartre, and both it and the square beside it are a sometime refuge for Parisians and visitors alike. It is possible to walk there, either up a great flight of stairs or by meandering along winding streets, but it is easier in the funicular! The square is surrounded by cafés, their brightly coloured tables spilling right across the cobblestones. It is a gathering place for painters, though only some of them are any good—I once sat in on the drawing of a child whose parents were delighted to pay almost any amount. The result was lovely—for them and for me!

Dinner on the first night of the tour was at one of those uniquely French restaurants in Rue Lepic leading to Montmartre. Our first-time visitors really knew they were in Paris when the first course of *escargots* arrived followed by *lapin* served with a delicious sauce. Some needed large gulps of wine to wash down the snails and rabbit, but none baulked at the different cuisine.

John and Anne were with me as the tour managers, of course, and on the second day they asked me to tell the group about my experience of living in Paris, a talk I called 'Living in Paris and loving it'. Those were very important years for UNESCO because the US and Britain had both withdrawn from membership and, as Australia's Ambassador, Gough had worked hard to keep Canada, in particular, and other nations involved. He was the Deputy Chairman of the World Heritage Committee and this was a time when many of the now famous listed sites were under consideration. I enjoyed my role in supporting him in these tasks, and particularly in meeting representatives from so many countries.

Of course it is often the simple things that stick most in your mind. I would tell the groups that in my free time during those years I loved visiting the great shopping complexes like Printemps or Galeries Lafayette and enjoyed the bus trips to these places—on my *carte orange,* a weekly bus and metro pass. I would also talk about my favourite Sunday treat of a subscription concert at the Théâtre du Rond Point, with musicians from near and far. Held between eleven and twelve-thirty, it was then possible to lunch very nicely in the restaurant below the concert hall. At other times we would travel home by metro or by bus, which I actually preferred, picking up fresh walnut bread, cheese and maybe some raspberries to go with the chicken casserole waiting in the oven. Such a good Sunday!

Australians visiting Europe for the first time often have unfounded fears that it will be very cold, but even in the coldest weather hotels, theatres and restaurants are warmed to a comfortable temperature, so we encouraged people to dress in layers, which would enable them to shed an outer coat or jumper if necessary. Thermal underwear can be a real hazard, a fact that was confirmed on one of our first tours in France when we arrived one cold night at a warm restaurant. Halfway through the meal one woman fainted. We got her to a private room where Anne, who is trained in first aid, routinely loosened the clothing around her neck. She then realised the apparent cause of the problem—the woman was being cooked. She revived shortly afterwards, though she probably still wonders how the thermal underwear she wore to the restaurant came to be in her handbag when she got back to the hotel.

We took the group to several museums, and made sure that they had time to visit the Louvre on their own—it is so big that it is hard to take a group through successfully. The Musée d'Orsay was the favourite for most of our people as it contains nineteenth and twentieth century French art. The ground floor has magnificent paintings and sculpture in more traditional styles. However, soon everyone migrated to the galleries of the French Impressionists. I always find myself lingering in front of the Renoirs, particularly his two paintings 'Country Dance' and 'City Dance'.

During the nineties I led four tours in France. On one of these we looked specifically at the Impressionist painters, spending time in Paris and Provence. Naturally we saw a whole range of the works of Renoir, Monet, Cézanne, Van Gogh and Matisse, and I was reminded to re-read Emile Zola's 'L'Oeuvre' (The Masterpiece) about the bitchiness of the art world in their time.

The Musée Marmottan is probably the best place to experience the art of Claude Monet, so naturally we made a visit. Paul Marmottan, an art historian, gave his nineteenth century family house, together with his paintings and furniture collection, to France in 1932. Then in 1971 Claude Monet's son, Michel, gave a huge collection of his father's works to the museum. They included the famous painting 'Impression: Sunrise' which gave the name 'Impressionists' to Monet and his contemporaries. A great many of the paintings in the water lilies series are at the Marmottan.

Other paintings in this series are to be found in the Musée de l'Orangerie, one of the small pavilions each side of the Tuileries gardens at the Place de la Concorde. Here you will also find well-known works by Renoir, Cézanne, Modigliani and Picasso. The lower ground floor has two rooms filled with what I call wraparound panels of the water lilies planted and painted at Giverny, Monet's house in the country. They never cease to delight, nor does the final part of my Monet tour—at Giverny itself. Here there are no original paintings, but there is a reconstruction of the studio in his charming provincial house, and the well-maintained gardens are enchanting.

On our first tours we stayed, as I have mentioned, at the Hotel Jardin de Cluny. Not only is it in the Latin quarter, but it is right near the Musée Cluny and the Panthéon. Other times we have stayed at the Hôtel Duminy-Vendôme and the Hôtel St James et Albany, both close to the Louvre on one side and the Madeleine and the opera house on the other. We always avoid the larger hotels that cater for bus-loads of tourists. Such hotels may be convenient, but they lack the special atmosphere that is Paris.

I have a friend from my days at the Australian Embassy, Alice Gay, who usually joined our groups for an evening out in Paris. Although she grew up in Sydney, Alice has been in Paris for so long that she really belongs there now. Indeed, she has a super little flat in the chic 7th arrondissement, just above the equally chic Rue Cler market. She loves the social and cultural life, and sings in one of the Paris choirs. It was Alice who suggested that we spend an evening on the *bateaux mouches*, those big boats which serve dinner as they move quietly along the Seine. The food is good and properly French. Paris looks so different from the river. There are grand floodlit views of Notre Dame and so many other buildings—the Australian Embassy looks quite noble!

No matter when one visits Paris there is always a range of theatre and music available. We usually managed at least one performance—and mostly they were very good. Opera is now only seen at the Opéra Bastille, and we took one group there for *Iphigenie en Tauride*, the story of the daughter of the Greek king Agamemnon. Iphigenie moved most uncomfortably around the stage on six-inch high platform soles. Betty, who found most things to be 'magnifique', was very concerned: 'That girl needs to see a good podiatrist', she said. I noted in my diary: 'Great performers; terrific sets; dramatic colours; peculiar production.' I must say that we have also seen some first class opera there. Ballet in the old opera house—the Palais Garnier, which has been beautifully restored—is an alternative.

Some of the better concerts in Paris are those presented in old churches. The Saint Chapelle provides a beautiful backdrop

and has excellent acoustics. We have attended some very memorable concerts in that church, usually just before sunset when
one can appreciate the depth of colour in the magnificent
stained glass windows.

For those who had not been to France before we tried to
include a visit to the Palace of Versailles. Arriving at the parking
area, the sight of several hectares of coaches patiently waiting
for their disgorged passengers prepared us for the disappointment that we would not be there on our own. In fact the Palace
of Versailles hosts more tourists each year than any other site
in the whole of Europe. So many visitors come in the tourist
season that only a small proportion of them manage to get
into the famous Hall of Mirrors. The enormous palace built by
Louis XIV is, by any standard, one of the grandest buildings in
the world and it's set in one of the finest gardens. It has also
been the scene of some of the most significant historical events.
It was here that the treaty ending the American War of Independence was signed in 1783. It was also here that the German
Empire was proclaimed in 1871 and Europe was restructured
at the end of World War I, culminating in the Treaty of
Versailles. No other palace in France has either the grandeur or
the historical connections which make Versailles a must to visit.

Another out of town journey that we have often included is
to Chartres and its famous cathedral. The present cathedral was
started in the twelfth century, although five other churches had
previously existed on that site. Its size and architecture are very
impressive, but the special attraction is the stained glass windows.
A luminescent blue glass, known as Chartres Blue, features in
the fine old windows. An Englishman named Malcolm Miller has
made a study of this cathedral his life's work and we have been

fortunate to have had him as the guide for our groups—not that he suffers any interruptions to his dissertations!

On our first tours of France we started our travels in Paris. We noticed that those who had not visited Europe before could feel rather overwhelmed by this wonderful but often frantic city. With ten million people it is the largest city in Europe, and more than twice as large as Sydney. Planning a later visit with the theme 'Heart of France' we decided to conclude, rather than start, in the capital. It would give our people the opportunity to get used to the French way of doing things before arriving in the great city.

On that tour we wanted to take part in the Anzac Day commemorations in the north of France, but to take advantage of warmer weather we preferred to travel in May. It was another good reason for concluding the tour in Paris. We flew into Charles de Gaulle airport and travelled immediately to Amiens, the main city of Picardie. The coach waiting for us at the airport was driven by Richard, whose only English consisted of the words 'no problem'. We communicated with him in French, but he really did have an amazing ability to understand us and what we wanted. We conducted many more tours in France, and always made sure that Richard was with us. He was an excellent driver, negotiating the sometimes tortuous roads without causing alarm as he took us around in his big white bus with blue and grey stripes on each side. I appreciated the little wooden step he produced to make climbing into the coach easier. Our groups loved him.

Richard had us at the Grand Hôtel de l'Univers in Amiens in time for lunch. The hotel had offered to prepare one sandwich for each person, and we'd wondered whether one sandwich each would be enough, but of course it turned out to be a very sizeable half baguette. Amiens is not on the itinerary for most Australian tourists, except near Anzac Day. It was the home of Jules Verne, author of those fascinating books we read in our youth, *Around the World in Eighty Days* and *Twenty Thousand Leagues Under the Sea,* so of course we went to see his memorial. The cathedral is a very impressive one and it has a chapel dedicated to Australian soldiers. We had a special interest in learning more about this part of France where Australians played a significant but tragic part in World War I.

Anzac Day is commemorated in France with many ceremonies on the Saturday closest to 25 April. The ceremonies are all held in the Somme, and Amiens is a convenient place to stay to take part in them. The Australian Ambassador to France usually plays a leading role while our Military Attaché has a primary responsibility, along with the local French representatives, for organising the ceremonies. John and Anne had let the attaché know that our group would be there and that we would have a priest, Father Jim, as one of the participants. We were invited to be involved in all the commemoration events. Father Jim was asked to officiate in the last two services of the day.

We had arrived in Amiens on a Thursday so were able to spend Friday on a tour of the battlefields. We visited nearly all the memorials to the five Australian divisions that had fought in World War I. Most people in our group had fathers, uncles or grandfathers who had fought there, and many of us could identify with names like Pozières and Moquet Farm. Nearly 60 000 Australian soldiers were killed in what was then called The Great War, the majority of them in this part of France.

On Saturday we left Amiens in time to arrive at the Australian

'Never forget Australia' it says—and the Australians will never forget their welcome at Villers-Bretonneux. With John and Father Jim.

memorial outside the small town of Villers-Bretonneux for the wreath laying ceremony at 10 am. This memorial covers a large area and contains the names of all Australian soldiers who were lost in France and who have no other marked grave. The view of the countryside from the tower at the back of the memorial is stunning, but it was desperately sad to stand there and look out over the fields where so many, including thousands of Australians, had died. In late April the wild red poppies are in appropriate profusion.

In the centre of the town is the French memorial and we adjourned there for the next wreath laying ceremony at 11 am. Australians had liberated Villers-Bretonneux during the war and all Australians remain heroes. We had been invited to attend the reception in the town hall, and this involved walking several hundred metres through the streets along with the friendly and applauding locals. The town hall has Australian animals carved into its woodwork, and there are signs saying 'N'oublions jamais l'Australie' ('Never forget Australia'). We felt welcome indeed.

Local school children here, and in some of the other towns we visited that day, are taught extensively about Australia and have links with Australian schools, such as Goulburn, in New South Wales. They sing Australian songs and they have competitions around Anzac Day for drawings of things related to Australia. After eighty years we are not forgotten.

Alice Gay from the embassy joined us on the coach to travel to our next appointments. First we had a big lunch in one of the village halls before going on to visit a high school which had a special Anzac Day display. Father Jim explained to Alice that he would like to conclude the prayers at the end of the last ceremony of the day by saying the Lord's Prayer in French. Like most of us Jim had learned French at school but was unsure of his pronunciation. Alice spent every available minute coaching him as we travelled along.

The second last event of the day was a church service in the village of Bullecourt. Ten thousand Australians had been killed or wounded in April and May 1917 in one of the bloodiest encounters with the enemy. Buried in the field where they fell are 2423 Australians. Father Jim donned his white vestments to assist the local priest with the service. His tasks included giving the homily and I will never forget his final words in that village church. He told of the church in the country town in Australia where he grew up, which had stained glass windows dedicated to French saints, St Martin de Tours and St Jeanne d'Arc. 'There in our church in Australia we have a part of France; here in the ground around your village you have a part of Australia.'

It was almost dark as the children of the village led us with flaming torches to the *Memorial in the Field*, just outside Bullecourt. This sculpture is of an Australian digger with his head bowed over his rifle as he stands in the field where thousands of Australians died. It was a sad service. Father Jim started the final prayers. Across the hushed and misty field we heard 'Notre Père qui est aux cieux . . . ta volonté soit faite sur la terre . . . délivre-nous du mal, Amen.' The bugler played the last post.

Most of our tours in France have included a few days in Burgundy, where we stay in the capital, Dijon. We travel there, from either Paris or Amiens, through fertile plains and rolling hills. Missing from the rural scene in northern France are farmhouses, for its history of conflicts has taught the farmers to live in villages and to travel to their farmlands. In late April and May the fields of canola flow as great golden carpets.

The bohemian heart of Dijon is the Place François Rude, named for a civic leader who did much to revitalise the city in the nineteenth century. Around the fountain in the middle of the square the locals gather to chat and drink coffee and wine. At the edge of the square are some fine fifteenth century buildings which now house restaurants. A favourite is Au Moulin à Vent, even though the stairs into it are rather difficult to negotiate and the angles of the floors, walls and ceilings are, to say the least, quaint. Many of those who have travelled with us have happy memories of rather good evenings spent there.

The palace of the dukes of Burgundy is just around the corner from the Place François Rude, but being in the centre of the medieval city the roads are narrow. The old palace is largely used as administrative offices now, with only a few rooms open for inspection. Opposite the palace, the Musée des Beaux Arts houses portraits of the dukes of Burgundy among the works by Flemish and Dutch masters and sculptures by François Rude.

The main boulevard leading through Dijon is Avenue Victor Hugo. The Hôtel la Cloche stands in Place Darcy at one end, and it is here that we always stay. It's a hotel with a lot of character, nice leafy courtyards and good service. It fits our constant aim of staying as near as possible to the centre of each city. Serving breakfast on our first visit to this hotel was a southern European waitress fussing around with coffee for her German, French and English speaking guests. A table of Australians no doubt had her confused. She poured coffee and politely asked, in a mix of German and French, 'Mit lait?'

While Burgundy as a region is now most noted around the world for its wines, Dijon is probably best known for its mustards. The former dukes of Burgundy established a culinary name for themselves by serving large quantities of various mustards at dinners when they were entertaining visiting dignitaries. There are some pleasing shops in the Boulevard de la Trémouille, many selling mustard and gingerbread. A more recent speciality of Dijon is the aperitif Kir, which was introduced by Canon Kir, Mayor of Dijon during the 1950s. At his civic receptions he always served a mixture of blackcurrant liqueur and white Burgundy wine, blackcurrants being another important product of Burgundy. When mixed with champagne it becomes Kir Royale. We took the opportunity of enjoying both versions. At home a mix of blackcurrant syrup and white Australian wine goes down well.

I've always been fascinated by the great Cistercian monasteries that were built throughout Europe. Many of them are now UNESCO World Heritage sites, although some are ruins. The rapid expansion of their numbers in the twelfth century was due to the charismatic leadership of a great theologian and philosopher, St Bernard of Clairvaux, who was born in Dijon. A short distance from the Hôtel la Cloche we found a statue of St Bernard, depicted as a small and humble man, in a square named after him. I was interested in taking the group to the memorial church built on the site of the house where he had been born in 1096. It is in a very old area on the outskirts of Dijon and access is by steep and narrow roads designed more for donkeys than coaches. A lesser driver than Richard would never have made it, but he managed to get us there. It was a visit that was inspiring for most but for some—like Father Jim, who knew Bernard's literary work and of his historical significance—it was a very special experience.

On our study tours we have included formal talks by local experts when this was appropriate. It was certainly the case in Burgundy, where we enlisted the help of Micheline Laby. Micheline is the author of two books—*Burgundy, The Magic of the Word* and *Dijon: A City of Art and History.* An elegant and friendly woman, her enthusiasm for the city and the region is quite infectious. She was able to place Dijon and the former kingdom of Burgundy in historical context for us. Starting in the fifth century she led us through to the time it became a duchy in the Middle Ages. She talked about the part the dukes played in the outcome of the Hundred Years War, and most other European intrigues, in addition to plying the monarchs with mustard. I'm sure that those who heard her will always remember the significance and extent of Burgundy, but probably will be unsure of the roles of Philip the Bold, Charles the Good and Charles the Bold. Or was it Charles the Bald (not to be confused with Wilfred the Hairy)?

Micheline also used to come with us for a full day's journey down the wine road of Burgundy. It is a journey through history as well as through colourful vineyards and fascinating wineries. My problem was associating the slopes with the right styles of wine and keeping up with her descriptions as we travelled. Our first stop was always the ancient winery of Clos Vougeot. This veritable castle among the vineyards had been a Cistercian monastery where St Bernard's monks made wine for many centuries. Their huge presses and other old wine-making equipment can still be seen. The great hall is used these days for the main wine ceremonial dinners of Burgundy. A coat of arms hangs above a high table with the motto 'Jamais en vain: toujours en vin' ('Never in vain: always in wine'). I like it.

For a visit to a working winery we would visit either Demeure St Martin or Le Patriârche. Both have extensive old underground cellars where a sense of euphoria comes merely from the sight and smell of the old French oak barrels. Gail Le Goff, with whom we became quite friendly over years of visits, would take us through the winery. We would stay for lunch in a restaurant attached to one of the wineries or in the town of Beaune at the end of our wine road.

Beaune's beauty lies in its winding streets and rambling buildings, many draped in the vines that bring fame and wealth

VINEYARDS EVERYWHERE—AND LOTS TO DRINK, ESPECIALLY IN THIS BURGUNDIAN WINERY.

to the region. It also has a strange tourist attraction, which I believe is unique among tourist sites of the world, the Hospice de Beaune. This institution dates back to 1443 following the realisation that Burgundy had backed the wrong side in the Hundred Years War. The hospice was built for disabled soldiers and the poor. The amazing coloured pattern in the tiled Gothic roof identifies it as a classic Burgundy building. It has now been restored almost to working condition. Thousands of people visit the hospice each year, the attractions being the buildings themselves, the wood carvings and the other works of art in the chapels. There is the sense that you have stepped back a few hundred years into an institution where the residents have just slipped out for a while so that you can have a look through.

My travelling companions were amused by the beds in the hospice. They were not much larger than one of our single beds, but each was for two patients or residents. After a wine-enriched lunch many of us rather felt like a nap and there was considerable mirth as we considered with whom we may have to share a bed. Our conclusion was that it was an interesting place to visit, but we were very glad indeed that we didn't have to stay there.

During our time in Burgundy we were made aware of many traditions unique to that region. It reinforced to us the idea that France is still a collection of regions with quite different histories, alliances and cultures. We were to see this even more in Provence, the area along the Mediterranean between the Rhône and Italy. It was a separate kingdom with a different Latin language until 1481. Provence, where we have stayed frequently, epitomises the regional characteristics of being slow and easy.

You get the feeling that Aix-en-Provence has been bypassed by much of the technology and population growth of the modern world. The fern and moss covered fountains that occupy central places in the Cours Mirabeau, the main street of Aix, ensure that the traffic moves slowly. Beyond this thoroughfare is a network of narrow streets and lanes with apartments, offices, shops and a more than average sprinkling of cafés. We walked up Rue Clémentine to Place Honoré, the heart of the medieval city, with its colourful fruit and vegetable markets. Here in the south there is a tendency for the siesta of other Mediterranean lands to continue. A long lunch befits the location—perhaps a Provençal salad of large green and black olives, hard-boiled eggs and a selection of excellent fresh vegetables dipped into a tasty mixture of oil and anchovies. Of course a bottle of Provençal wine is essential—rosé for me.

It was not chance that took Paul Cézanne and other Impressionist painters to live in Aix-en-Provence. Some say it was the light, others the climate or the lifestyle. Certainly we have always enjoyed visiting Cézanne's studio. It is in a pretty house at the top of a hill, only a short distance from the town centre. There is a view to his beloved Mont Saint Victoire. The studio gives the impression that Cézanne will be back at any moment to complete the painting on the easel. So many of the objects used in his paintings are scattered around, such as the apples and leaves lying on the windowsill, as they were when he painted that memorable scene of his own studio. Since many of his works were very large, their removal was facilitated by a slot built into the back wall of the studio—a useful innovation.

To appreciate Cézanne's work a drive to the countryside around Mont Saint Victoire is equally rewarding. It's like travelling through his paintings, particularly if the sun is shining on the red and orange earth and it is the season for red poppies. There is also an excellent guide to a good walk, *In the Footsteps of the Painters,* available from the tourist office in Aix. It leads us past the painting school as well as the apartments and favourite cafés of Paul Cézanne. I have enjoyed taking this walk with my travellers.

We went to St Rémy de Provence where Van Gogh had been confined to St Paul de Mausole asylum. It is peaceful and beautiful and here, away from the stresses of life, Van Gogh was able to produce some of his now famous works. 'The Sunflowers' and *La chambre de Van Gogh à Arles* (the original is in the Musée d'Orsay) were among these.

THIS NOTRE DAME HAS A REALLY HAUGHTY OUTLOOK. IN MARSEILLE WITH SOME OF THE GROUP.

The biggest city in Provence (and the second biggest in France) is Marseille. Its history goes back to the Greek and then Roman dominance of the Mediterranean, particularly because of the attraction of its port. Unlike Aix, technology and population growth have made their presence felt in Marseille. It is worth visiting even if only to see the old port, where the smells and sounds have remained unchanged for centuries. We would also take our groups to the basilica of Notre Dame de la Garde for further viewing of the enchanting Mediterranean.

Leaving Marseille we travelled to Cassis, the prettiest of coastal towns. Excellent restaurants on its sandy Mediterranean shore all offer a splendid bouillabaisse. To dine there on a pleasant evening, looking out across the sea, is a sheer delight. When we planned to take our first group to Cassis, Gough assured me that the soup would be full of fish bones. I think he was envious of our visit. As we had a mobile phone with us I took pleasure in phoning him at home in Sydney from the coach, as we left after dinner, to assure him that the superb meal was not spoilt by bones.

Northwest from Provence our coach headed for Sarlat in the Dordogne for our next headquarters. It was easy to tell that we had arrived in the Dordogne because of the dramatic change in the terrain. The Dordogne River has cut a huge valley through the limestone plateau. It is an area of rich green countryside with some truly fairytale castles and great scenic rewards. Sarlat is a pleasant and knowable small town with some wonderful medieval streets and buildings. I was looking forward to finding my way around the town and exploring the countryside.

One of the couples who were with us in France, Alison and Robin, lived in Sydney, where Robin worked as an actuary. Robin is very quiet, Alison isn't. They are an erudite pair, never flaunting their knowledge, but they have a quite encyclopaedic comprehension of a great range of topics. I enjoyed their company on this tour and have been delighted every other time they have travelled with us.

Alison and Robin sat beside our faithful driver, Richard, for dinner one Saturday night while we were in Sarlat. Richard slipped out of the dining room, returning a short time later with serious news for them. Alison stood to give us all a translation: 'It has just been announced that Jacques Chirac has been elected President of the Republic of France.' As she finished speaking a car passed by, its horn blowing and its occupants cheering wildly. Other cars followed in quick succession, the people in them showing similar jubilation. The celebration continued into the night. I couldn't understand why a presidential election would bring so much rejoicing to the whole town—surely some would have voted for other candidates. Wandering along the street after dinner I commented to one of the locals that the election of a new president had caused a lot of excitement. 'Presidential election?' he said with astonishment. 'Sarlat won the football!'

The rugged landscape of the Dordogne created some unique sites which were developed in medieval times as defensible towns. We had a wonderful day exploring them. One of the most interesting of those was Rocamadour, which is actually built on the side of an almost sheer cliff. Nice place to visit but it would be terrible to live there. A less well known town is Domme, perched right on the edge of a precipice. It is not as touristy as Rocamadour and it has a little train to transport one around—good for weary feet.

Each region of France has its own cuisine, of course. In Burgundy it is boeuf bourguignon, which is served ad nauseam to all visitors. In the Dordogne the specialty is goose liver pâté or foie gras. The local guide could not understand why a group of Australians did not want to see the farms where they force feed the poor geese. They also produce many ducks in the region and a favourite way of preparing the *canard* is to roast the rolled breast in a berry sauce. The roasting is minimal and the resulting dish could be described at best as medium rare.

When we had dinner at Les Chevaliers de la Tour in Sarlat, one of our group informed the waiter that there was no way he was going to eat meat like that. He wanted it properly cooked. The waiter obligingly returned it to the kitchen and brought it back later almost black, a state of cooking that our participant obviously enjoyed. A few nights later we were to have duck at a different restaurant. Knowing of our friend's preference, we asked the chef beforehand if we could have one meal well done. It must have lost something in the translation for the chef looked at us blankly. 'Canard à la Jeanne d'Arc,' someone suggested. He grinned knowingly and later provided a very well roasted specimen. By the time we left the region I noted in my diary: 'I think I've had enough duck for a while.'

Before returning to Paris we were to stay in the Loire Valley, which may have the greatest claim to being in the heart of France. No part of France, perhaps the world, has such a rich heritage of castles. The Dordogne has some pretty castles, but in the Loire they are grand. My favourite is Chenonceau, which was built in the sixteenth century and combines grandeur with beauty and some sense of intrigue. It forms a bridge across the River Cher, and includes many impressive halls and rooms. Chenonceau is notable for having two separate wings each embellished, during the time of Henri II of France, with formal gardens. One was designed by his wife, Catherine de'Medici, and the other by his mistress, Diane de Poitiers! Another intriguing part of the history is that in World War II Chenonceau was used as a hospital and as a bridge for the exchange of people between a divided France.

On days when we travelled longer distances we often organised a picnic for the group. We have done this in many countries of the world, but it was probably easiest to prepare in France. For thirty people we would buy sixteen or eighteen baguettes, a kilo or more of ham, a couple of the local cheeses and some tomatoes. Cornichons added the final touch. Wines of the

HEADS DOWN FOR A QUICK FEED IN THE FRENCH COUNTRYSIDE.

region, some still mineral water—what more could one want? Maybe mustard? The whole group would help prepare the picnics, buttering bread, slicing tomatoes, opening bottles of wine. Richard soon learned the sort of places we wanted to go—off the road, beside a shaded creek or with a lovely outlook over the countryside. It was more difficult to find a table to prepare the food, but somehow we would manage with a park bench or low wall.

On our first tour we kept noticing a small car that seemed to be following us, day after day, with the same attractive driver. Eventually the penny dropped—this was Richard's partner. She did catch up with him each evening but did not want to intrude. When we realised the situation we welcomed Silvie warmly into our group activities. Silvie and Richard really enjoyed our picnics and on the last day before we returned to Paris they announced that they wanted to provide the picnic for us all. It was much as we usually had it, but a little spicier. In a quiet chat I had with Silvie she told me that she and Richard were 'trying to make a baby'. Following our first tour Richard bought a large folding table and took it with him on the coach for use ever after. But there was no news about a baby arriving.

When I think of France and dream of visiting there again, a picnic on the grassy bank of a stream with my travelling companions is a must. Then in my mind I travel down the wine road of Burgundy. I drift back to Paris with its grand boulevards, browse through a favourite gallery and then sit sipping coffee at a café round the corner from 'home', wherever that happens to be at the time. Yes, France will always be dear to my heart.

CHAPTER 2

THE RED FLAG FADES

TREMENDOUS POLITICAL AND social changes took place in Russia during the 1990s. I had the privilege of travelling there on several occasions, which was exciting but often sad. Some of the other countries that had been behind the Iron Curtain fared somewhat better than Russia. The red flag, the symbol of Soviet domination, was fading.

I led a group tour through Prague, Dresden and Berlin when many of the most dramatic changes were taking place. Prague still had little crosses in Wenceslas Square commemorating those who had died in the uprising only a year earlier. Dresden seemed to be in a state of confusion coping with the change of allegiance from east to west. The Berlin Wall was still coming down. We were in Berlin when we heard the news that Leningrad had returned to its original name of St Petersburg.

On that tour we stayed on the top floor of a twenty storey concrete and steel hotel in the former East Berlin—not uncomfortable and with great views over the entire city. An incident on our first night there reminded me that I needed to have an open mind about the things we would experience in Eastern

Europe. After dinner I was waiting for the lift with Betty, who had been with us in France, and some of the others. One woman was complaining that she had a terrible view from her window. 'I look down and all I can see is factories and the railway shunting yard.' 'How sad to get such a bad room,' said Betty. 'From my window I can see right across the city with gardens and steeples and other lovely buildings.'

I stayed to chat to Betty after the others had left. Looking down the rooming list I commented to Betty, 'You are in the room next to the woman complaining about the view. You have exactly the same view!' Betty simply gave one of her wonderful smiles.

Before we'd finished that tour we decided that a longer trip through Eastern Europe to see the incredible changes taking place would be very worthwhile. On our return to Australia I talked to Gough about the idea of him joining me to share leadership of a tour to Russia and other parts of Eastern Europe the following year. He warmed to the idea. It became the first of ten tours that we led together. Several of them were into Eastern Europe.

The following May our group of thirty gathered in Vienna, with the leadership team of Gough, Anne, John and me. We started the journey east—down the Danube by ferry for our first stop in Bratislava, at that time the second major city of Czechoslovakia. A year later it was to become the capital of an independent Slovakia.

Bratislava is a city with a former glory. For more than a hundred years it had been the capital of the kingdom of Hungary when Budapest was occupied by the Ottomans. When we arrived it was obvious that the harshness of the postwar years had left much of the city dirty and broken. During the days of the Iron Curtain many rather gross concrete and steel buildings were erected on the outskirts of expanding cities like this. The old structures in their centres were left unharmed. Often they were falling to ruin through neglect. At least they didn't rip out the hearts of their cities to rebuild, as often happened in the west.

Prague is another of those cities. On our visits in the early nineties I could see the start of its resurrection as one of the world's loveliest. It was to be our next stop after Bratislava. Our Prague 'home' was the Hotel Ambassador in Wenceslas Square, which is not so much a square as a boulevard. This is a grand old hotel in a first class location and within easy walking distance of most of the old city. It took quite a few years for the hotel to be brought up to scratch, but we have since enjoyed many nights there and eaten some wonderful meals in its restaurants and cellar.

On our first visits there was an *automat*, or workers' café, just near the Hotel Ambassador. It was great fun to line up for a delicious sausage with mustard and a big glass of Czech beer. This all had to be consumed standing up, while happily exchanging smiles with the locals. The cost of such a meal in those days was about forty cents, depending on the weight of the sausage. The newer eating places soon learned to charge standard European prices.

Music is the soul of the Czech lands, as it is through all of Central and Eastern Europe. I really love the deeply moving sounds of the composers Smetana, Dvořák and Janáček as they rallied the spirits of the Czechs over the years. The country has continued to produce first class performing musicians as well.

One experience was to show that the administrators of the theatres are not of the same class as the performers. Prior to our visit we had arranged to take the group to a symphony concert. When we arrived in Prague we were informed by the box office that the concert had been cancelled, but there were tickets for us to see the ballet *Swan Lake* at the state opera house. That evening we sat in the opera house, the lights dimmed and the orchestra started playing the overture to *Madame Butterfly*. Murmurs of surprise came from the audience all around us, but no one was disappointed with the performance we saw that night.

We travelled on through the territory that, until a year before, we had known as East Germany. The first city after crossing from Czechoslovakia is Dresden, once regal and beautiful. It was almost completely destroyed by Allied bombing in 1945. I cannot accept that it was justifiable to bomb a place of little strategic military significance in those last days of the war.

The ruins of the Frauenkirche in Dresden have been left as a ghastly memorial. Ironically the church was untouched in the bombing, but the heat of the fires around it set alight archival films stored in the crypt, so that the whole church was also completely destroyed. Prior to the war it had housed a magnificent display of paintings of the city of Dresden by Canaletto, the great eighteenth century Italian artist. Fortunately they had been removed to a secure place during the war and are now in the nearby Semper gallery. I found it quite stunning to see the detailed city scenes. It had indeed been a beautiful city.

It is difficult to obtain accommodation in Dresden. On this tour we spent the day in Dresden, but had to take accommodation at nearby Chemnitz. Many of the signs in the city still referred to Karlmarxstadt, the name it had been given after the postwar division of Germany. It had only just been re-named Chemnitz shortly before our visit. We were on unfamiliar territory there and the lack of contact between East Germany and Australia became apparent when we arrived at the hotel. John, who is a Whitlam-like six feet three inches, went with Gough and me to the reception desk to check the group in. The receptionist was looking a little strangely at the three of us. John asked if they had had many Australians to stay. 'You are the first Australians I have ever seen,' she confessed. 'Are *all* Australians as tall as you?'

The journey from Dresden to Berlin took us through one of the great environmental disasters of unwise industrialisation. For mile after mile we travelled through pine forests which were completely dead from acid rain. The trees, still with branches intact but no green to be seen, were standing in the dreadful silence. Other remains of those difficult days were the 'Trabbies', the East German produced Trabant cars. Those that were still going belched black smoke from their exhausts, but most were not going. On country roads there were dozens of them simply abandoned where they had died. In the towns and cities we learned of the human anguish as the files of the Stasi, the East German secret police, were opened. People were amazed at the information that had been recorded, and they were shocked to discover who the informers had been— neighbours, friends and even family members.

A plane journey from Berlin to Moscow eventually got us to the heart of Russia. Moscow airport is quite a good introduction to the city. It was dark and the luggage trolleys clang along, if they work at all. The officials can be very intimidating.

Eventually we gathered the group together outside despite the milling crowds. It was there we met Mariana and then everything was all right.

Mariana is really most charming and personable. Mid-life and full of life, she is a cultured woman with a love of Russian history and the skill to share her knowledge in an interesting and memorable way. She is an expert organiser, and that gave us great confidence. Such a gentle and attractive person. Not only do I admire and respect her, but I became very fond of her. My appreciation and affection were shared by all of our people who travelled with her.

During those early visits we stayed at the Hotel Rossiya, a huge grotesque building with one of its four sides facing on to Red Square. Mariana managed to get us all rooms on the side looking out over St Basil's Cathedral to the walls and gates of the Kremlin. The rooms were falling to pieces, but while the curtains in the bedrooms may have been tattered, the view and the location were unsurpassable.

Sometimes in the evenings people from our groups would slip across Red Square to watch the guard changing on Lenin's tomb. The guards' feet would snap to attention in time with the last stroke of the hour from the great Kremlin clock. Peter Egan, who led a number of music tours to Russia for us, told me about the night his group went to watch the changing of the guard the year following our first visit. They watched the new guard arrive to take up positions beside the old guard then, as the clock struck the hour, the old and new guards marched away together. They discovered the following day that they had been among the few to witness the historic event of removing the guard permanently from Lenin's tomb.

In later years the conditions in the Hotel Rossiya were such that we could no longer take our groups there. The rooms had deteriorated even more and sleazy mafia types haunted the corridors and foyer. We had to take our groups to more upmarket hotels, which usually had foreign management, even though the locations and views could not compare with the Rossiya.

Every visitor to Moscow wants to see the Kremlin, and I doubt if anyone is disappointed by a visit there. It's the old walled fortress where the early Tsars lived securely with their extended families and courtiers. It includes grand palaces and three beautifully designed and decorated cathedrals. When Peter the Great moved the capital of the empire to St Petersburg at the end of the eighteenth century, the Kremlin remained his Moscow home and was used for other administrative and ceremonial purposes. Lenin moved the administrative capital of the USSR back to Moscow and the Kremlin, so that it became a synonym for Soviet power.

The Armoury, within the Kremlin, is a place I find quite breathtaking. Instead of storing weapons there, the Soviet leaders made it a museum to display the enormous wealth of the Tsars. Fine jewellery by Fabergé contrasts with large but lovely carriages. Also located in the grounds of the Kremlin are the largest bell in the world (it broke before it was rung) and the largest cannon in the world (it was never fired). I think there may be something symbolic about Russia in these two huge devices. I found the collection of smaller cannons left behind by Napoleon in 1812 of particular interest because of their historic significance.

Equally as memorable as the grand buildings of the Kremlin were the visits in Moscow which brought us in touch with ordinary Russian people. One morning we had had the option of dividing into three smaller groups to visit either a school, a hospital or a collective farm. Lunchtime back at the hotel was a buzz as people compared notes.

Meg, a high school teacher from Sydney, told us about the school visit. All the children, in both primary and secondary departments, learned English as part of the standard curriculum. She told us how, as in schools everywhere, some keen girls sat in the front seats while the boys who would rather have played sat at the back of the class. They had met the Deputy Principal, who was responsible for the English teaching program. He had never been out of Russia but could speak with an English, American or even an Australian accent on cue. The whole group was delighted and very impressed with the motivation of the pupils and staff.

By contrast, those who had been to the hospital came back saddened. Lillian, one of the doctors in our group, told of very primitive conditions in the cardiac hospital they had visited. Four nurses on each shift cared for seventy patients. The medical equipment was twenty years behind the equipment used in a comparable Australian hospital. The facilities were rundown and the doctors didn't have the basic necessities, such as bandages and medicines, to treat their patients properly. We could only share her dismay.

Kenneth returned from the collective farm impressed by its organic nature, particularly as Moscow's water supply came from that area. General maintenance on the farm was poor, there was concern about falling crop yields, and there seemed generally to be an atmosphere of despondency among the farm hands. Kenneth thought that there was a great oversupply of manpower and very low productivity compared to farms similar to his in Tasmania.

One evening we had another opportunity to break into smaller groups, this time to visit some Russians in their homes. Of course we were limited to places where at least one member of the family could speak English. The six in my group went to a tiny flat in the suburbs in one of those large, rather ugly edifices found everywhere in Russia. Victoria, Oleg and their son Alexander were all musicians—father often away conducting, mother home teaching, son still a student practising on the piano that filled their living room. Alexander, a very bright sixteen year old, also slept in that living room. It was where the family cooked, ate and entertained. One small bedroom and a minute bathroom just fitted off the entrance hall. Nonetheless, we received the warmest welcome with a jolly supper helped along by wine we had brought. Alexander gave us a fine performance of music by the Russian composer Scriabin. They were a good family and they endeared themselves to us.

Gough went to the home of a university mathematics teacher. Anatoli lived there with his wife and daughter, who was in her late teens. Their flat consisted of three small rooms plus a tiny bathroom and a smaller food preparation area. The smallest room was used by their daughter as her bedroom. The second smallest was Anatoli's study, his bedroom and also the place where he kept the family transport—a bicycle. The living room, which at night was converted to his wife's bedroom, was filled to capacity when six Australians sat around the dining table. Anatoli told them that in the communist years he had the money to travel abroad but was never permitted to do so. Now he was free to travel but had no money. He told of being able to read

Hemingway's *For Whom the Bell Tolls* only after someone had smuggled a copy into the country and duplicated it. Anatoli's was the sixth carbon copy and he read it in secret, sometimes under the blankets with a torch. From his shelf he took down the encyclopaedia published by the state in the 1970s and read aloud the entry about Australia—'a puppet of the United States'. Gough was amazed to discover that Russians could read in the encyclopaedia about himself—'Prime Minister and leader of the workers' party'.

Mariana told us that when she worked as a guide in the Soviet era she had to report each night to a KGB agent about the people in her group of foreign visitors. 'What is their attitude to the Soviet Union? Are any communist sympathisers?' Mariana was glad that era was over.

One of the delights of being in Moscow is having the opportunity to visit the Bolshoi theatre. Many people identify it with ballet but it is home to both opera and ballet companies. When Gough and I were there twenty years earlier the orchestra played *Advance Australia Fair* in honour of having Australia's Prime Minister present—the first time that our new anthem had been played in that famous theatre. With our first group tour we were looking forward to a performance and were especially thrilled when Mariana told us that she had been able to get tickets for Gounod's *Faust*.

It was a dazzling night. Singers, orchestra, set and lighting were brilliant. Marguerite's arias were glorious and 'The Soldier's Chorus' was spine-tingling. Gounod had written a full ballet sequence for the middle of the opera, but this is rarely included today as it needs full opera and ballet companies. That night we got the lot with the number one cast, including star dancers recently returned from a European tour. As we descended the main stairway on our way out, a member of our group who was walking behind us asked what we thought of the opera. Gough stopped on the steps, turned around and announced, a bit pompously but sincerely: 'That is the greatest theatrical performance I have ever seen.'

Our practice of arranging to have speakers and seminars during the tours proved very rewarding in Moscow. One afternoon we had Professor Spartak Beglov from the Department of Political Science at Moscow University. He is the father of one of the delegates to the International Conference on Adult Education which I had been involved in organising in Australia a few years earlier. As well as teaching at his university he was a regular commentator on the national television network. Through the years of perestroika and glasnost, and then through the break-up of the Soviet Union, he had nightly explained to the Russian people what was involved in these great political, social and economic changes. He told us that Gorbachev made the mistake of bringing too many new people within his circle. His consequent dependence on them and their fear of removal led to his isolation. I liked this man's openness and the way he reached out to communicate with us.

By the time we finished the tour in St Petersburg, Gough was ready to continue travelling with ISP groups. People obviously valued his background talks and interpretation of the things we were seeing. He found that he had a great opportunity to witness current developments and to learn. Two years later we were both back in Russia to lead 'The Great Russian Journey'. It would take us from the Pacific Ocean right across the country to the Baltic Sea.

Although Vladivostok is well known as the terminus of the Trans-Siberian Railway it is not so easy to get to. It has always been the main Pacific port for Russia but in the years of the Cold War it became a major military base and so was off limits to tourists. Instead of Vladivostok we chose to enter the Russian far east at Khabarovsk, a big city to its north. To get there we flew to Tokyo and then took the bullet train to Niigata on the western side of Japan. Aeroflot took us into Khabarovsk. It sounds complex, but doesn't take that long.

Flying into Khabarovsk we saw the city of over 600 000 people spread out along the great Amur River, which connects it to the Pacific. This is one of the largest cities in Asia which has a predominantly European population. The view from the ground as we landed was less impressive than it was from the air. Hundreds of ailing aircraft were parked around the perimeter of a rather tatty airport. A dilapidated bus rattled out to take us to the grey terminal. We had to search for immigration and customs forms written in a language we could understand. I started to wonder about the wisdom of us being there.

As we passed through the official exit we were suddenly in a different world, with the sound of balalaikas and a blaze of colours. A Russian folk group was there to welcome us. A lass stepped forward from this reception party with bread and salt. We were being given the warmest Russian welcome. And, best of all, there beside the team of musicians and dancers was the smiling face of Mariana. I was suddenly very glad and I knew that this journey would be a wonderful experience.

We were soon settled in our hotel, with introductions being made all around as most of us had not met before we left

Australia. Dinner started with a glass of vodka, then the four courses were washed down with Russian champagne. The travellers in our group were quickly getting to know each other, which was important as the three weeks ahead would not always be easy-going.

It certainly was an interesting team that gathered that night in Khabarovsk. There were engineers, doctors, teachers, a psychologist, a builder, a farmer, a newsagent and a number of successful business people. There was a young journalist who, these days, I hear regularly reporting on the ABC from cities around Australia. There was Father Jim, whom you met in France.

We were glad that Dr Hugh was with us. His presence gave me a great sense of security in a country where we had little faith in the local medical services, and at times were to be distant from any Russian medical assistance. Over the years of travel Dr Hugh has been a great help and has handled a number of medical crises that occurred along the road. Hugh and his wife Elfie have been great company on their many tours with me because of their easy-going manner, sense of fun and concern for other travellers. You will meet them again as we travel.

One of the difficulties we had in arranging tours in Russia in those times concerned paying our bills. Before the break-up of the Soviet Union, everything had been handled by the state-owned Intourist. Now some of the hotels and other services wanted to be paid in cash. Our partners in Moscow had asked us to bring sufficient American currency to pay our way through Siberia. That's how Anne came to walk off the plane carrying a bag with US$30 000 in it. And that's why John walked at her heels. It had been such a large amount of cash that we had to declare it when leaving Australia, and the officials at Khabarovsk wanted to know why we had so much and what we were going to do with it. They even insisted on counting it. Khabarovsk is noted as a centre for organised crime and I didn't like the idea of us having so much money with us. The arrangement was that Anne would pass the money to Mariana as soon as we arrived. 'Later,' said Mariana when Anne first tried to hand it over. It was a little nerve-wracking seeing this anonymous bag being passed between Anne and Mariana regularly for the next week. 'Mind the bag,' Mariana would call as she threw it to Anne before going off on some errand.

Few Australians would bother to visit Khabarovsk if it were not such a convenient place to join the Trans-Siberian Railway. It is a typical Russian city, solid buildings and wide streets, and it is almost as close to Australia as it is to Moscow. The streets are broad and it has some fine brick buildings. The Amur River is so wide here that it is difficult to see the bank on the other side. It carries a constant procession of barges loaded with containers or piles of minerals. I walked along the river in the early morning and saw some very big fish that had been pulled in by the local amateur anglers.

We joined the Trans-Siberian early in the afternoon for one of the great train journeys of the world. We filled two carriages, which were to be accommodation and conveyance for the next two and a half days. We were to travel as far as Irkutsk in the heart of Siberia. While I really loved this journey on the train, I found that the distance we travelled was quite far enough for me. The full length of the railway is twice the distance from Sydney to Perth and takes seven days. One would have to be a great train enthusiast to take the full trip.

MY FAVOURITE TRAIN CONDUCTOR, VERA.

Each carriage has an attendant to care for the passengers. Ours was an indomitable lady named Vera, rather more attractive than most. She'd been on the job for twenty-five years and took her work very seriously, unlike those seen loafing in some other carriages. She brought us cups of tea and coffee or hot water with which we could make our own soup, and she really tried to keep the carriage clean and comfortable.

Meals were served in the restaurant car, which involved quite a walk through the lurching train and they were adequate though not enticing. In Khabarovsk we had been given cucumber with each meal and thought that it must have been the favourite local vegetable. On the train we continued to be served cucumber at every meal—not just a few slices, but a solid section as big as a tea cup for each person. Our group was consuming more than ten metres of cucumber a day. It turned out that we ate ten metres every day for the rest of the trip. The dark bread was rather hard and stale when we boarded and it became less edible at each meal. We were the only foreign passengers and I noticed very few Russians cared to eat in the restaurant car. I was soon to discover why.

In each carriage there was a notice indicating where and when the train would stop and for how long. The stops, sometimes up to thirty minutes, occurred every few hours, and we came to look forward to them. Vera would smarten her uniform and place her cap firmly on her head before helping us off the carriage, telling us each time not to be late back to the train. The platforms were only raised a foot or so from the ground although they were often twenty metres or more wide, and on every one of them there were dozens of food stalls, mostly operated by older women selling their home-grown and home-made produce. This, I now realised, was how the Russians travelling on the train obtained their meals.

We learned to enjoy the extras available at the stations. The hot baked potatoes and the apple fritters were just what we needed. At one of the stops John discovered a woman who was selling fresh bread, so he bought a loaf and took it along to the restaurant car for our lunch. It was a great improvement on the stale dark bread we'd been served until then. At the next stop quite a few of our people, unbeknown to each other, went searching for bread sellers. There was great amusement as the fresh bread was piled higher and higher in the restaurant.

Gough was particularly interested when the train stopped at Petrovsky Zavod. This was one of the places where the Decembrists had been exiled after the uprising against the Tsar

MAN MUST EAT, AND APPLE FRITTERS ARE THE GREAT ATTRACTION AT A WHISTLE STOP ON THE TRANS-SIBERIAN RAILWAY.

in December 1825. On the station platform was an impressive monument erected to them, with pictures of their leaders. The Decembrists were aristocrats and army officers who brought music, education and culture to Siberia at a time when most of the others exiled there were poor and uneducated people.

The theoretically egalitarian Soviets didn't like to refer to 'first' and 'second' class, even in relation to their trains—they used the words 'soft' and 'hard' instead. Each compartment in soft class, where we travelled, had two beds, one either side of a central table. They were quite comfortable and I slept well each night. Perhaps a little vodka and a song or two with a few of the group crowded into the compartment in the evening helped make the bumping less noticeable. In hard class there were four beds in the same space. The most serious deficiencies on the train were the scarcity of water and the toilets.

The latter were very old style, which we had decades ago in Australia. Despite Vera's best efforts at keeping ours clean it was still rather repulsive. John and Anne had brought along some bottles of eucalyptus oil and at least that camouflaged the smell. Nell, who was in the compartment near mine, brightened the loo by leaving a little ditty for us: 'If you sprinkle when you twinkle, Be a sweetie, wipe the seatie.' I must say that almost hourly it evoked some new piece of doggerel from one of the others in our group.

The real value and enjoyment of travelling through Siberia by train is the scenery. Most of us have visions of the Siberian land-scape as bleak. Certainly from the train in the warmer months that is not so. There are rivers and streams, green pastures and birch forests. Drawn from my book, I would look out the window to see the quaint villages, timber houses with blue window frames, sometimes a little cemetery in which each grave was surrounded by its own miniature iron fence, painted blue.

Late in the afternoon on the third day the train followed the southern edge of Lake Baikal, the largest freshwater lake in the world. In some places sheer red rock rises from the water while in others, the water laps against grass or a sandy beach. Siberia has probably the richest reserves of minerals and other resources in the world. In this lake alone is one-fifth of the world's fresh water. In a land of great natural wealth is terrible poverty; with its beauty there is grim harshness. I was still pondering the enigma of Siberia when we arrived at Irkutsk. It was 1.30 am and the end of our train adventure.

We stayed in a hotel where Aleksandr Solzhenitzyn checked in later in the day. The Nobel Prize winning Russian author, who had been exiled for writing about some of the horrors which took place under the old regime, was returning to live in Russia after twenty years in America. Unlike us, he remained holed up in his room during his stay. We were soon out exploring the city and enjoying the restaurants, bars and shops. Irkutsk has a good feeling about it and has some wonderful nineteenth century timber homes and public buildings. It is also the administrative capital of Siberia. The embankment of the Angara River attracts hundreds of locals and visitors each evening to promenade as people do in Italy and France. The local artists display their pictures there. Some call Irkutsk the Paris of Siberia. One evening Mariana announced that she was going swimming in the river and invited us to join her. Only one man accepted her invitation.

As well as having Mariana to guide us through the whole journey we would often have the services of a local guide. Yuri was in his early twenties. He had been born in Irkutsk, knew all about it and proudly thought it was the centre of the world. 'It is an important city,' he explained. 'From here you can go west to Moscow, east to Khabarovsk and south to Mongolia.' He didn't mention that if you go north you arrive pretty quickly at the North Pole.

For the next leg of our journey we did go west, but only as far as Ekaterinburg in the Ural Mountains. We could have travelled there by train, but after two and a half days on one I was now glad to be flying. Ekaterinburg had been a closed city for many decades. It was one of the main areas for armament production and out of bounds mainly for that reason. The Soviets also didn't want people to make a pilgrimage shrine of the place where the last Tsar and his family had died.

Ekaterinburg, named for his second wife, Catherine, was

established by Peter the Great as a 'window to the east'. He had already established St Petersburg as a 'window to the west', naming it not directly for himself but for his eponymous saint. The old road to Siberia passed this way. We went just out of town on that road to the top of the Urals and stood with one foot in Europe and one in Asia. In the days when English convicts were shipped to Australia, Russian convicts were forced to walk to Siberia. As they passed this marker, where we now stood, they would weep.

After the Russian revolution the name of the city was changed to Sverdlovsk. Concurrent with the opening of the city to visitors only a year before our visit, the name had been changed back to Ekaterinburg. The manager of the hotel, the local guide and the KGB agent, who had all come to check us out, assured us that we were the first group of Australians to arrive since the city had been opened.

Our hotel would probably rank as the most rundown I have ever stayed in, although it was the best in the city. Soon after we checked in our travellers gathered in the lounge with stories about their rooms—holes in the walls, plumbing that didn't work and broken furniture, to name a few of the common problems. Members of the group had bonded on our train journey across Siberia and they could see the humour in staying at this hotel. This was, after all, one of the costs of spending two days in a city we were all eager to explore. We gave the participants some comfort by arranging for a bottle of vodka and two bottles of champagne to be provided on each table at dinner. We all slept well.

The local guide was keen to take us to the modern city that had been developed as Sverdlovsk. Certainly the commercial and industrial areas and the university are large and impressive. He also wanted to show us the home of the man who had invented the steam engine and another who had invented the bicycle! He couldn't quite understand our greater interest in seeing other things, such as the relics of the first Russian foundry and mint, established more than two hundred years earlier by Peter the Great. There was an unusual museum devoted to cast iron work—in its former days of great craftsmanship Ekaterinburg foundries produced amazing artistry in iron.

We particularly wanted to see the site of the 'house for special purposes' where on the night of 16 July 1918 Tsar Nicholas, Tsarina Alexandra, Olga, Tatania, Marie, Anastasia and Alexei the Tsarevitch were gunned down in the basement. We knew that on the orders of Boris Yeltsin, who had grown up in Ekaterin-burg and become the administrator of the region, the house had been levelled. A strange silence came over our group as we arrived at the site. There is a wooden cross above where the fateful cellar had been. An old man had appointed himself as the custodian of the site. He knew of Gough and solemnly presented him with a photograph of the Tsar. A small wooden chapel had been erected, the first step towards building a permanent Orthodox church dedicated to the man whom many Russians regard as a martyr. We felt the sadness of that place.

We flew on to Moscow where the changes since our previous visit were obvious. Streets were being dug up and renewed. The central department store, GUM, was alive with a hundred specialty outlets selling consumer goods from around the world, and strung around the entrances to the metro stations were long rows of people trying to sell some family treasure, a flower or a bottle of cola. There were no longer queues of people waiting

At the memorial to the slain royal family, a custodian presents EGW with a picture of the Tsar.

to visit Lenin's tomb, though his embalmed body was still there, albeit unguarded.

We had a seminar in the Kremlin which was rather special. As well as the tour that Gough and I were leading, another ISP tour group was in Moscow at that same time. This second group, led by former ABC Moscow correspondent John Lombard, was to join us for this seminar, which meant that we had nearly seventy people. We had asked our partner company in Moscow if they could arrange a large room for a seminar. 'Perhaps in the Kremlin?' we had suggested, a little tongue in cheek. To our surprise they faxed back to say that they had obtained a room for us in the Kremlin. It was the one used for new ambassadors to present their credentials.

Chairing a meeting in the Kremlin was rather a thrill for Gough, and I must say he performed well. The first speaker was our Australian Ambassador, who gave a very lucid explanation of what was happening in Russia from an Australian's perspective. It was also good to hear John Lombard talk about his days in Moscow during the cataclysmic events of 1991.

We went to yet another great performance at the Bolshoi. This time we saw the ballet *Giselle.* On the way out I had somehow managed to get ahead of Gough. I waited outside the theatre with others from our group. When Gough arrived at the main staircase he was greeted by waving and cheering crowds that followed him right out the front door. Naturally he responded warmly. When he joined us we were able to tell him that the bald head beside and just below him was that of Mikhail Gorbachev. You would have thought that at least he might have recognised the birthmark!

Memorable in a different way was the *a cappella* choir which sang in the church of St Barbara on the edge of Red Square. I love music sung this way and I acquired several new CDs. To hear a good choir in an ancient church in the heart of the country adds real soul to the experience. One of the men travelling with us wrote later about the tour: 'I was looking forward to hearing music in Russia, but didn't realise that at times it would raise the hair on the back of my neck and on one occasion I would be in tears.'

One afternoon we visited Peredilkino, a romantic village in the woods on the outskirts of Moscow. Boris Pasternak had lived in a comfortable house there for the last twenty years of his life. Much to the caretaker's distress I leaned on the desk where Pasternak had written *Dr Zhivago*—and was admonished

RIVERSIDE ARCHITECTURE IS JUST SO DIFFERENT.

vigorously. We also went to Leo Tolstoy's town house, which was much more grand. The atmosphere in his house was such that as we walked around, it seemed as though we might meet Anna Karenina or someone from *War and Peace* in the hallway or in the next room. These old houses really are alive.

The tour was to conclude in St Petersburg, but on the way there we had several days to cruise down the Volga River. Ancient cities on the Volga like Yaroslav, Uglich and Kostroma are where the Russian state began a thousand years ago. They predate Moscow by three hundred years and St Petersburg by seven hundred years. It was fascinating to walk along the towpaths where the boatmen had once heaved the barges while singing their mournful songs. We stopped at the many little stalls for handmade shawls and scarves.

The cruise boat would stop at one of these historic cities during the day, casting off again in the late afternoon. The days were long and we were able to sit at dinner watching the green banks drift past. Sometimes we would see the golden cupola of a church and know that a village was hidden from our view. The meals on the boat were good, tasty and plentiful—the borsch was especially memorable. The dining room was presided over by an impressive woman whose blonde hair was wound on top of her head. Some of our group suggested that, with her senatorial looks and bearing, her name might have been Bronny.

St Petersburg at last. Such a different city to Moscow—the canals, the grand boulevards, the graceful bronze statues, the buildings in the style of Western Europe. Peter the Great built it not only so that he could trade with the west but so that he could bring western ideas into his empire. I love to drive down Nevsky Prospect, the grand boulevard which surpasses many in Western Europe on which this one was modelled. I cherish memories of the Winter Palace when viewed from the opposite side of the Neva River.

I must always go into St Isaac's Cathedral in St Petersburg to see its arches and the dazzlingly restored mosaics on the walls and roofs. The malachite columns in their brilliant marbled greens are wonderful. More sombre, but impressive in a different way, is the cathedral in the St Peter and Paul Fortress. It is here that Peter the Great and the Tsars have been buried. When we visited there was a place reserved for Nicholas II. His bones have since been added.

Following the Western European tradition, the Tsars built summer palaces outside the city. The grandest is Catherine's Palace at Tsarkoe Selo. It is similar in design to the Palace at Versailles, though not as large. However the soft blue coloured walls and the golden domes make it far more beautiful. It was occupied by Nazi forces during World War II when they besieged St Petersburg for 900 days. Much of it has been restored to its original condition and I always enjoy another look. After the official tour of the palace we wandered around the stalls in one of the halls where various Russian souvenirs were sold. Suddenly Gough came looking for me. 'Come and see Hawkie,' he called. Our group of Australians had found a man selling quill pens and, yes, he did have a remarkable prime ministerial resemblance. They say we all have a double somewhere.

The tour was coming to an end. I had noticed that our man who went swimming with Mariana in Siberia was increasingly with her. He was a doctor, unattached, and about Mariana's age—they made a nice couple. I saw the meaningful glances that passed between them. By the time we arrived in St Petersburg they were definitely an item.

Our last full day of the tour was a Sunday. In the morning we went to the Hermitage, a part of the grand Winter Palace, which houses one of the world's most valuable collections of art. The building itself, with its imposing staircases and rooms decorated in different styles, is a great work of art in its own right. Some of our group stayed there during the afternoon. Others went to shop! Father Jim headed for St Catherine's Church for a late mass.

That evening we had planned a farewell dinner at a restaurant called the Senat Bar. The coach to take us there was waiting at the door of the hotel. We counted the group on board and found we were one missing—Father Jim. Just then a taxi arrived with the dilatory reverend. His brother priests at St Catherine's

QUITE A FEW VODKAS WERE CONSUMED HERE—SUMMER PALACE OUTSIDE, WINTER COMFORT WITHIN.

had welcomed him warmly—and with more than a few glasses of vodka.

I have spent some pleasant evenings in St Petersburg, but none as joyful as this night at the Senat Bar. The food and drink were excellent. There was a group of folk dancers to entertain us, and that they did incomparably. Perhaps it was a sense of joy mixed with a certain relief to be coming to the end of a demanding but really fabulous tour. There were a few tears—including Mariana's, of course. We concluded with some speeches, all very much from the heart, from the leaders and some individual members of the group. Father Jim leaned over to John, who was chairing the function, and whispered, 'Would you like me to say a prayer?' John paused and then decided that those in the group would like the dinner to finish that way. There was no indication of Jim's wayward afternoon. He prayed warmly for the Russian people and their leaders in this time of change. There was gratitude for our safe journey, and the experiences along the way. Even a word for the relationships bonded within the group and between Australian and Russian people. Amen, I could say to all of that. When we arrived back at the hotel, Jim fell off the bus.

With good humour Dr Hugh and some of the others helped him to his room. It was the time of the White Nights—the sun sets but it doesn't really get dark. Some felt that it was too good a night to waste in bed. Next morning we were bustling to make our departure straight after breakfast. Anne was standing at the bottom of the stairs checking off each person as they came down. 'That was a wonderful prayer of yours last night, Father Jim.' 'What prayer?' he said in surprise.

We were soon on the long flight home. Back in Australia some months later we were delighted to have a visit from Mariana. The romance was blooming. The following year we announced to the others who had been in that group: 'Mariana is going to marry your former travelling companion. The date for the wedding has been set.'

Russia is a place of mixed emotion for me. It has a beautiful but strangely cruel landscape. I am fascinated by its cities; I thrill to the beauty of its music and art; I feel deeply for its people. Many of them have lived their entire lives through constant difficulties which no one should have to endure.

3

BRITAIN IS GREAT

I LOVE VISITING ENGLAND. Scotland is romantic and beautiful and also the home of my ancestors. And who could not be delighted by Wales? Really—Britain *is* great.

Our first group tour to Britain was designed as a literary one. It was one I planned to lead on my own, English literature having always been one of my passions. However, when Gough saw the itinerary he realised that we were going to places he would love to visit or revisit, and he kept dropping hints that he would really like to come too. I relented and John and Anne agreed that he could come along. He would already be in Europe at that time anyway. But I was still to lead the tour. Famous last words, they occasionally proved.

What better way to start a literary tour than in Poet's Corner of Westminster Abbey? We stood among the graves of Chaucer, Dickens, Dr Johnson, Browning, Tennyson, Hardy and Kipling. There are memorials to Shakespeare, Bunyan, Wordsworth, the Brontë sisters, Robbie Burns, Lord Byron, Adam Lindsay Gordon and dozens of others familiar to us. I find a certain satisfaction in discovering memorials to those who are particularly significant to me.

We were soon headed south to Canterbury, where our hotel was The Chaucer, in Ivy Lane. The Lord Mayor of Canterbury and the Lady Mayoress joined us for dinner on the first evening and welcomed us warmly to Canterbury and to England. Dick wore his chain of office and Joy her chainette. At first I thought they might have been stuffy, but they were kindly and interested in our mix of professionals, housewives, farmers and public servants. Dick spoke of the many attractions of the city and its little known son, Christopher Marlowe.

When Thomas à Becket was murdered in Canterbury Cathedral in 1170 he was soon made a saint and Canterbury became a place of pilgrimage. The setting for the *Canterbury Tales* is a group of pilgrims travelling from the Tabard Inn, near London, to Canterbury. Mine host from the Tabard led the group and each pilgrim told a story to pass the time as they travelled. To experience something of Chaucer's pilgrims we arranged to walk along that part of the Pilgrims' Way which comes across the South Downs into Canterbury.

It was lunchtime when we arrived at a little pub at Boughton Lees. As we spilled out the door of the bus our enthusiastic guide emerged from the door of the inn dressed as a fourteenth century pilgrim. 'Welcome to the Tabard,' he called. 'I'm the host of the inn and I'll join you on your pilgrimage to Canterbury.' We all thought it was rather fun. The path led off across the fields, over stiles and through woodlands. Some of the cottages along the way had been resting places for pilgrims for hundreds of years. Our host had cast some members of the group as Chaucer's characters—the Knight, the Wife of Bath, the Prioress—and had given them short versions of the relevant tales, so at the first stop the Knight told his tale, and so on as

THE 'KNIGHT' TELLING A TALE ON THE PILGRIMS' WAY TO CANTERBURY.

we travelled. Each 'pilgrim' loved the experience and it was certainly a great way to travel to Canterbury.

Right beside the cathedral is the King's School, a collection of ivy-covered buildings, some of which were part of the original monastery on this site. The school was established by Henry VIII. The library at King's is named for Somerset Maugham—his ashes are located there with an appropriate memorial plaque. I arranged for us to visit the library to see the Maugham memorabilia, and the librarian pointed to a school photo. 'I believe that two of the boys with Somerset Maugham had connections with Australia,' he said. Checking the names we worked out the trio. One was Howard Mowll, who went to China as a missionary and eventually became Archbishop of Sydney. The other was John Gellibrand, who became a major general in the Australian army and a knight of the realm with outstanding service at Gallipoli and in France.

Later he served as Public Service Commissioner in Tasmania, Police Commissioner in Victoria and was a Member of the Australian Parliament. Maugham himself became the novelist and playwright often remembered for the time he spent in South East Asia. I looked at the innocent faces of the three schoolboys in the photo. No one could have predicted their futures, trials and fame on the other side of the world.

Winchester in the south of England was our next stop on this journey. In the main street a quite modern equestrian statue of the Saxon King Alfred reminded us that it was here he ruled as king of all England. As this was a literary tour I pointed out that Jane Austen spent her last days in a house near the cathedral and that she was buried inside the cathedral. There would be time to visit both places.

I went with some of the group to the cathedral. Gough went later on his own. When I returned to the coach in the afternoon Gough was already there. I could see that he was agitated. 'Margaret,' he said, speaking almost in awe, 'I don't think that all our people have appreciated what we have just seen in the cathedral!' Then a few moments later he asked, 'Would it be all right if I made a short presentation on the bus?' It was the only time on the tour that he had made such a request so I agreed that he could carry on.

Gough took the microphone quite smartly. 'Fellow travellers. Many of you would have found your way to the nave of the cathedral. You would have seen the caskets with the remains of King Canute and a number of the other pre-Norman kings of England. I found it very moving to be there with those relics.' Starting with King Egbert and Alfred the Great he recounted details of the monarchs that had ruled England up to the

Norman invasion. Then, with the arrival of William the Conqueror in 1066, he outlined how the Danish dynasty had married into the Norman line, thus linking the pre and post conquest families. He was rattling off dates of coronations and marriages as well as describing the significance of each event.

I looked around the coach. I think everyone was listening to every word, but I knew that he had not had the opportunity to check his facts. I noted that we had three high school history teachers in the group as well as a history lecturer from the University of New England. For nearly an hour he spoke, hardly pausing to draw breath, and I feared the group would boo with impatience, but as he came to a close they all, historians included, burst into loud applause. It still amazes me that he can recall so many dates. I mused on the fact that he has trouble remembering his own telephone number . . .

There is something else that gives me particular satisfaction in Winchester Cathedral. It has the elaborate tomb of Richard Beauchamp, Fifth Earl of Warwick, who was one of those involved in the 'trial' of Joan of Arc in Rouen in 1431. With poetic justice a lovely and delicate statue of Joan has been placed high in the cathedral where she looks down on the tomb of one of her tormentors.

By Winchester we were into 'Hardy Country', although nearby Dorchester is where Thomas Hardy mostly lived. 'Shaped as if by a kindly hand', he wrote concerning this peaceful, undulating part of England. We saw houses where he had lived and churchyards and buildings that he wrote about—places 'far from the madding crowd'.

Travelling through Devon and Cornwall the literary connections span centuries and flooded into each day. The home and study of Agatha Christie are interesting to visit, though no murder has ever taken place there. On windswept Dartmoor one expects to see Sherlock Holmes and the hounds of the Baskervilles appear at any moment. The real Jamaica Inn is just as Daphne Du Maurier described it in her novel of the same name about smugglers. Is Tintagel King Arthur's Camelot? After our visit there I like to think so. And Lyme Regis was the perfect setting for John Fowles' *The French Lieutenant's Woman*, as well as for Jane Austen's *Persuasion*.

Most of us identify Jane Austen with the gorgeous Georgian city of Bath, yet in reality Jane lived there for only a few years and there is so much else to commend the city.

We have organised many tours to Bath. One of the reasons for the success of those visits has been an association with a superb organiser and guide, Jane Glaser. Jane is the daughter of one of Bath's leading surgeons and her mother had read the entire works of Jane Austen while pregnant—hence the name chosen for their newborn daughter. We sometimes think Jane believes that she *is* Jane Austen. I think there are many similarities—she has a sharp wit, is perceptive, has never married, is always composed, and has a beautiful speaking voice.

Not only has Jane looked after every group that we have had in Bath, but one year she led a three-week long 'Jane Austen' tour for us. It was just after the run of Jane Austen films had been on television and in the theatres. She took the group to so many places that are referred to in the novels or where recent filming had taken place. Some, like Mr Darcy's 'Pemberly', are open for anyone to visit. To visit others not open to the public, Jane used her extensive connections.

One nearby place that Jane took us to on our first tour was the Australia Chapel in St Nicholas Church at Bathampton. 'It was built in memory of Admiral Arthur Phillip,' she explained. Admiral Phillip? Of course in Australia we only know him as Captain Phillip, the first governor of New South Wales. That was his rank when he came to Sydney in 1788, but afterwards he was promoted to admiral and that is how he is remembered in Bath. My group loved visiting the chapel, particularly because there is a strong presence of Australia—emblems of the Australian states adorn the walls, Australian timbers have been used in the furnishings, and the kneeling cushions had been embroidered by the women of Hobart Cathedral.

Another special experience in Bath was our visit to the house at number 4 Sydney Terrace, where the Reverend George Austen and his family lived, and where we took tea with the present owners. The house is kept as it would have been in 1805 when the Austens lived there. We enjoyed the cucumber sandwiches and Mrs Perrot's Heart Cake, a recipe handed down by the Austens.

Every visitor to Bath should see the Roman baths. There are the eighteenth century 'modern' baths, but more fascinating are the now underground Roman ruins. We took one group for a private evening visit, and found it to be quite an eerie place without the tourist crowds. When we came up to the Georgian baths that night there were large flaming torches mounted in sconces, high on stone pillars, casting reflections in the water and bringing the statues to life with their golden light. Here was a truly elegant scene—dinner was served for us at three round tables, each illuminated by tall white candles burning in silver candelabra. The food and wine were delicious.

I must hasten through the Cotswolds, that range of green hills rolling down through Gloucestershire and dotted with villages where each honey-coloured cottage is often further beautified by climbing roses. As well as visiting the Shakespeare houses in Stratford on Avon, I have always been keen to attend at least one of the great man's plays at the Royal Shakespeare Theatre. We have stayed at the White Swan Hotel in Stratford, where the creaking floors and low ceilings are part of the ambience and provide a direct link to Elizabethan times. On other tours we have stayed instead in Banbury at the Whatley Hall Hotel. Banbury Cross, where we rode in our childhood imaginations on a nursery rhyme cock horse, is just outside the hotel. The hotel boasts that Jonathan Swift wrote much of *Gulliver's Travels* while staying in room 29. From Banbury it is easy to travel up to Stratford for an afternoon or evening performance, and it is a good place for visiting Oxford and many of the well-known gardens such as Hidcote.

Throughout the nineties we organised twelve tours which spent all or part of their time in Britain, but I have been mostly writing about experiences on that first literary tour. Five years later we planned what would have been my last group tour in Britain. We called it 'Great Experiences of Britain with Margaret Whitlam'. All the arrangements had been made, my suitcase was packed and ready. Ten minutes before pick-up time I was tidying the living room, quickly rolling up some cords, when suddenly I tripped over one and came crashing down on my already twice-replaced hip. Being home alone and in great pain it was fortunate that I could just reach the portable phone lying on a nearby table. This is where it pays to remember phone numbers, for I was able to ring my GP who rang everyone else. Mind you, security at our place is so complete that I had to wait till my daughter arrived with keys to let everyone in, including the ambulance officer who took me away to St Vincent's Hospital. A woeful way to spend three weeks promised to others. It was little compensation to find the break was only the pelvis—I still couldn't walk!

John and Anne stepped into the dual roles of leaders and managers of the tour. My son Stephen, who was joining the tour, was able to take the bad news, together with the maps and notes I had prepared, to the airport. Every few days I would phone my group during their enviable journey. The dear participants kept a diary for me, with a different person recording the events of each day, and Stephen reported on the whole tour. I was more than disappointed, finding the experience quite stressful as several other health problems followed the fall. However, let me include some of the experiences of people who did make that tour as we continue our journey clockwise around Britain.

Wales has a special fascination for me. My father's family name was Dovey, a Welsh name, and some years ago I had lunch at the Dovey Hotel in the little town of Aberdovey—as had my parents before me. Many coal miners came to Australia from southern Wales and it is moving to visit the mining villages in their ever so green valleys. We have built up a good relationship with The Royal Oak hotel in Betws-y-coed in the north of Wales and that is where most of our groups have stayed. Betws is a village in a narrow but most idyllic valley and trees thickly line the small river which flows right past the hotel with its contrasting old black and white walls. Mr Kavanagh is the stout publican who runs a very cordial and well-organised house from the kitchen—and the food is excellent.

One day my group visited the great Castle of Caernarvon, which sits at the far northwest of the Welsh mainland. It was begun in 1283 by Edward I to a grandiose design, and is in a strategic position at the end of a chain of castles which Edward constructed along the north of Wales. They saw, as had I many years before, where the investiture of the Prince of Wales still takes place. The highlight of the afternoon, however, was to go by track railway to the summit of Mount Snowdon. It is the highest mountain in Wales and higher than any in England. It is almost always shrouded in mist and that day was no exception, but that did not detract from this great little train journey.

That evening they dined at Plas Newydd, home of the Marquess of Anglesey. Pre-dinner drinks were served on the terrace above the beautiful gardens which run down to Menai Strait. On the other side of the water was the national park and the now perfectly visible Mount Snowdon. After dinner the sky was still as clear as crystal, the North Star hanging like a wonderful jewel over north Wales.

One of the great traditions of Wales is its male choirs. There used to be one in every valley and even in these times of change and competing interests, there are still many of them. The men take their task seriously, meeting for a practice or a performance at least twice each week. We arranged for the Moelwyn Choir to come to the Royal Oak one Sunday night to sing for our group.

The Moelwyn choir, which had twenty-four singers, was conducted by a woman and another woman played keyboard for them. As our dinner was concluding the group became aware that the choir was gathering in the bar outside. John went out to talk with them. One man identified himself as the leader and explained that he would introduce the singing. 'The conductor's name is Sylvia Jones, the accompanist is Wenna Jones and I am Glyn Jones,' he explained. 'All from the one family?' John asked. The tone of the answer indicated surprise at the naivety of the question. *'Noo,* we're not related.'

The choir gathered at the end of the dining room. Jones the Choir Leader read the list of songs they would sing. 'And if you are a good audience we can sing an encore,' he concluded. Jones the Conductor had them singing in beautifully controlled but expressive harmony. We must have been a very good audience indeed, for after much applause they sang two encores. 'Cwm Rhondda' was sung first in Welsh then in English, with the familiar words 'Guide me O thou Great Jehovah', so that the Australians could join in. They concluded with 'Land of Our Fathers'—the Welsh national anthem, a song which brings a tear to many eyes.

A tour in Wales must include Tintern. My group went there the day after the choir sang for them. Driving into the deep valley through oak, ash, maple and beech, the ruins of Tintern Abbey rise in delicate arches of surprise. When Wordsworth visited here he wrote of 'these beauteous forms . . . that on a wild secluded scene impress'. As my group walked among columns in the great church, through the refectory and the ancient chapter house, they were easily able to imagine that the White monks of Tintern were there with them.

The Cistercian community came here in 1132. There were already monasteries of other orders in Britain, usually in the settled areas such as Canterbury and Westminster, but the Cistercians chose 'places away from men' which, in cases such as Tintern, were also breathtakingly beautiful. When visiting

Tintern I am reminded of the simple beginnings of St Bernard of Clairvaux, who was responsible for the development of the order, in a humble home on the outskirts of Dijon, which we had visited on our tours in France.

Places of beauty abound in Britain, but few can compare with the Lake District in the northwest of England. Our groups have usually stayed at The Old England on the banks of Windermere at Bowness-on-Water. The landscape bewitches with its green hills rising from placid lakes—rivulets flowing by stone-walled fields, sheep with black faces and long shaggy fleeces, roads winding through majestic valleys. In fact there is a whole vocabulary of Lake District words for the countryside, like 'fells', 'pikes' and 'becks', which are as poetic to us as they are descriptive to the locals.

When we visited the Lake District with our literary tour we had a wealth of interesting places to see. Most famous among the Lake poets is William Wordsworth and his presence there in the early nineteenth century was a stimulus for Coleridge, Southey and De Quincey to join him. Thomas Arnold, with his more famous literary son Matthew, had a house nearby to the Wordsworths for their summer holidays, while Sir Walter Scott was among the many visitors. John Ruskin, the Oxford professor who wrote on social issues, came to live in the Lake District, as did Beatrix Potter, and it was here that she created or discovered her characters such as Peter Rabbit and Jemima Puddle-Duck.

Rydal is the focus of the Wordsworth connection in the Lake District, in particular a rambling country house called 'Rydal Mount', where he spent thirty-seven years, the longest period of his life in any one place. He planned the garden, which is still as he intended it, and bought a field nearby for his daughter, Dora. There he planted hundreds of daffodils, which still grow in profusion. He chose the site 'to build, within a vale beloved' the little Rydal Church. The Wordsworths, including William, the poet laureate and church warden, always sat in the front left pew of the church. The Arnolds, including young Matthew, sat in the front right pew. We could sit in the second row and imagine the great poets to be just in front of us.

Most visitors seek Wordsworth connections in the larger, better known, Grasmere. In fact the family spent thirteen years in Grasmere in two different houses, one of which they disliked. William is buried in Grasmere because the hillside site he chose for the Rydal Church is a solid rock outcrop and it is not possible to dig graves there. After his funeral at Rydal they took his coffin on a horse-drawn wagon to the graveyard in the softer ground of Grasmere.

'Rydal Mount' is open to the public each day, and it is a joy to see. On one of our tours we arranged a private evening visit. The manager, Peter Elkington, showed us around the gardens, by the croquet lawn and then through the house. Wordsworth's study, with its outlook across the lake, is a treasure. We gathered in the living room for wine and gingerbread—Lake District specials.

Peter asked if one of our group would read a poem. We nominated Mary, who is a teacher of English and history at a high school on the south coast of New South Wales. She is a confident person, well experienced in the classroom and with groups, but she found the next few minutes rather unnerving. Peter showed Mary to a rocking chair, William Wordsworth's own favourite chair. He handed her a sheet and soon she was reading to us: 'I wandered lonely as a cloud That floats on high o'er vale and hills, When all at once I saw a crowd, A host of golden daffodils.' It was a magic few minutes and the group listened almost in awe.

The contemporary playwright Alan Ayckbourn has his own theatre at Windermere. He converted an old laundry into an intimate theatre 'in the round' and named it, appropriately, The Old Laundry. We took the group there to see a performance of *Table Manners*, a homely little story raising issues about our society and values.

An incident during the interval nearly brought the play to an unexpected climax. It had been a warm evening and most of the group had succumbed to buying an icecream from the enthusiastic young seller who walked through the theatre. We were then each left with a wrapper and stick in hand. Gough thought that he would be helpful and found a waste paper bin at the front—actually on the edge of the stage. He kindly took the bin to each member of our group and collected the papers and sticks, then returned the bin to the front. When Gough sat down John waited a little while then quietly took the bin outside and emptied it in a more appropriate place. Thank heavens, for during the second act one of the actors grabbed the bin in the course of the drama and flung it in such a way that, had the papers and sticks been where Gough had placed them, they would have showered the cast and the audience.

I would linger longer here, but I should take you on to Scotland. For one of our tours we flew into Aberdeen to commence our journey through Britain. It was the city of my maternal grandfather and I was delighted when the Lord Provost, the Scottish equivalent to a lord mayor, invited the team to the Council House for a reception. Aberdeen had just elected Margaret Farqhuar, the first woman to hold the position. The group felt very honoured to be received in such a grand manner.

Aberdeen is notable for its clean-cut, grey granite buildings—the whole city is built of it. It is also famous for its maritime traditions and in fact my family came from the nearby fishing village of Portlethen. Fishing and now North Sea oil have made the seaport very important.

We were also invited to Aberdeen University, one of the oldest in Britain, where our travellers became students and Dr Jennifer Carter treated us to an illuminating lecture around the theme of the university's motto: 'To serve truth and society together.' She mentioned some of the graduates of the university who over the centuries had made outstanding contributions to world affairs. Some were well known, but others were less familiar—such as Henry Farqhuarson, who established Peter the Great's naval academy in Russia. Others had helped establish universities in America, Hong Kong and Australia. Another had become governor of Queensland. One of their research scientists had discovered the relationship between malaria and mosquitos—and so the list went on.

Aberdeen is the gateway to the Scottish Highlands and we were able to experience something of the charm of that countryside. I wanted to take the group to Crathes, now a National Trust property. It is an excellent example of a Scottish castle, with six foot thick walls and beautiful gardens. Because of the savage effects of the north winds in Scotland, they have used great hedges to create protected areas for shrubs, flowers and even vegetables. We continued up the River Dee to where we could get glimpses of Balmoral Castle. A visit to the Lochnagar Distillery left a good taste in the mouth! This really is Scotland.

Now is probably a good time for me to introduce you to another of our regular travellers. You will meet him not only in Britain but in other parts of *My Other World*. Charles was born in the north of Scotland in the town of Nairn. 'The bairn from Nairn' is his own light-hearted description of himself. Proudly still a Scotsman, he moved to live in other parts of Britain, then to Russia and other countries as a representative for a chemical company, and finally settled in Australia. Great man to have on a tour, particularly to Scotland but also to other countries where he has lived, as his knowledge of local customs is very helpful. In Scotland he was able to assist us in understanding what almost seemed a new vocabulary, and he introduced us to such things as haggis with tatties and bashed neaps.

Charles is a gentleman. When I first met him on another of our tours I was impressed by his stature and good humour. A warm round face, but above his face nothing that required any attention by a barber. He was a widower who sometimes cut a lonely but dignified figure among the group. Charles commented that Aberdeen, like Queen Victoria, was stately, moral, well educated, prosperous and ornate.

When we travelled from Aberdeen to Edinburgh we called at Glamis Castle. Charles assured anyone in doubt that the correct pronunciation was 'Glams'. Glamis, the childhood home of the Queen Mother, is a regal and historic castle, warm and lovingly cared for.

On this tour we stayed for four days in Edinburgh, home of a now revitalised Scottish Parliament. This allowed plenty of time for a proper walk up the Royal Mile and around Edinburgh

Castle, as well as visits to gardens, galleries and the Princes Street shops.

The castle is well known to people around the world because of the widely televised Edinburgh Military Tattoo. Its rugged outline on Castle Hill dominates the city. Most of the interior of the castle is harsh and cold—designed for soldiers in defensive roles. Naturally my favourite place there is the tiny chapel dedicated to St Margaret, the Hungarian born princess who married Malcolm, King of Scotland. It is partly hewn into the rock of the castle mound and the rest completed in thick stone slabs. While the exterior melds into the hard dark rock of the castle, the interior is painted pure white. It is so small that a dozen or so people would fill it completely. There is always a bowl of flowers in the chapel, provided and arranged each week by a different woman who has the given name of Margaret.

One of the great visits out of Edinburgh is to St Andrews. It is not a large town, but lays claim to a number of significant historical events. It is best known as the home of golf and the location of some of the most famous golf tournaments. Although I've visited St Andrews several times with my Scottish cousins, I have not yet managed a game of golf there. But I do remember on early visits taking tea at the course and being overjoyed to drive through Dr Findlay's Casebook country on the way to St Andrews.

The origin of golf dates to 1754, but this is late in history compared with some other notable events at St Andrews. It was around 360 AD that St Rule arrived with a bone of St Andrew the Apostle—hence the origin of the name of the town. An abbey was founded and Scotland's first university established in 1410, the third oldest university in Britain after Oxford and Cambridge. John Knox was a student at that university and the first moves towards the Reformation in Scotland were taken here. We always take our groups to dine in the Golf Hotel in St Andrews. It looks out over the Royal and Ancient Golf Course and also the beach where Olympic runners trained and the beach scenes for *Chariots of Fire* were filmed. As we returned to Edinburgh on the coach our people were still talking about their surprise at seeing where so many interesting and significant events had taken place so closely together.

We travelled down through the Scottish Borders region. We had a brief stop and very special treat when the group was entertained by my friends George and Davina Portarlington. George and Davina are the Earl and Countess of Portarlington and their estate, Gledswood, has lovely fields and woods. In the manor house we took an afternoon tea of cakes, tarts, scones and, of course, shortbread before heading off across Hadrian's Wall and on to the magnificent city of Durham. Both are wonderful places and there are stories I could tell of the group visits there. But stop for a while in York we must.

On the literary tour we spent several days in the magical city of York. The city itself is an omnipresent joy with its famous Minster, its almost complete city walls and wonderful old streets. The narrow Shambles is the best known, but the surprises are in the underground recreation of Viking dwellings. It was in York in 306 AD that Constantine was proclaimed Roman Emperor, one of the most significant appointments in the history of the world.

We went out to Haworth, best known as the home of the Brontë sisters, Charlotte, Emily and Anne, and where their father was the vicar. The old vicarage looks out over the tomb-stones and tall trees of the churchyard, and it is easy to feel drawn into the plot in one of the eerie scenes from *Wuthering Heights* or *Jane Eyre*. Although it is right beside the industrial city of Bradford, Haworth retains its pre-industrial revolution charm. We had lunch at the local pub—a large pie-shaped York-shire pudding covered with delicious gravy.

To see the world of a modern writer we took the group one afternoon to Thirsk and the start of the Yorkshire Dales. Alf Wyte, who wrote the very popular books and TV series *All Creatures Great and Small* under the pen name of James Herriot, was still in his veterinary practice at the time of our first visit. His surgery has since been turned into a museum. The room where he saw his animal patients has been left as it always was and the living rooms are just as they were when the vets used them. The Yorkshire Dales are really one of the prettiest areas of Britain.

Britain has wonderful theatre in its regional centres, and so we grasped the opportunity of seeing a first class performance in York. The Theatre Royal there is an excellent venue and we were fortunate in being able to take our literary lot to see a performance of *Rebecca*. We'd all read Daphne Du Maurier's book and seen the 1940 Academy Award winning film starring Laurence Olivier and Joan Fontaine, but the stage play in York brought life and action to the story in a delightfully dramatic way.

The road from York to Nottingham passes Sherwood Forest where Robin Hood and his merrie men had lived among the old oak trees. We stayed in a hotel in Nottingham near the castle. Nearby was the Olde Journey to Jerusalem Hotel, which had been carved into the castle rock in the days of the Crusades.

MODERN DAY CRUSADERS WITH BRIAN GRAHAM.

A modern day statue of Robin Hood stands beside it. The program here for our literary tour had been arranged by Brian Graham from the Adult Education Department of the University of Nottingham. I had met Brian at the International Adult Education Conference in Sydney some years before and I certainly appreciated his efforts in making our Nottingham visit such a memorable one.

D.H. Lawrence is the novelist most readily associated with Nottingham, although in fact he grew up in nearby Eastwood, the setting for his earlier and best known novels. We went out to Eastwood on a cold and misty afternoon. We pulled up outside a row of terrace houses which immediately seemed familiar from Lawrence's description of his hero's home in his largely autobiographical *Sons and Lovers*. 'Is this The Bottoms?'

I asked, referring to the name of the terrace in the novel. Brian smiled and nodded. It is a row of miners' cottages built at the bottom of the hill, but in those days it was separated from the rest of the town by a large open field.

We went on that same afternoon to visit Newstead Abbey, the former home of Lord Byron. In a comparatively short lifetime he produced much splendid poetry. There is a good museum in the grand house where we learned more about his world, including his fatal attraction to Greece. Though a couple of generations apart in time, the homes of Lord Byron and D.H. Lawrence were only a few miles apart. The contrast in their two worlds is enormous.

The Sheriff of Nottingham invited us to the Council House. This is a handsome Georgian building in the main square of the city. There has been an unbroken line of Nottingham sheriffs for more than a thousand years and, courtesy of Robin Hood, it is one of the best known public offices in Britain. Just before 10 am we mounted the grand stairway of the Council House, were shown to a large room and asked to sit in the chairs around it.

At the stroke of ten o'clock one of the Sheriff's men came to the door. With that commanding voice which seems to be mastered only by the aides to royalty and other dignitaries in Britain, he called: 'Ladies and gentlemen, please stand for the Sheriff of Nottingham.' I looked to the door and then around the group. Eyes were wide open and faces showed various expressions of surprise. What was immediately obvious to the group was that back in the days when Robin Hood roamed Sherwood Forest, the ancestors of the present sheriff were in Africa.

MEETING THE SHERIFF OF NOTTINGHAM.

The sheriff is a distinguished civic leader who plays his role with dignity. He is a warm person and we found that he and his wife were a lot of fun. After welcoming us all, he called formally for Mary, the poetry reader, to come forward. Nervously she answered his summons. 'Happy birthday,' he exclaimed and planted a kiss on her cheek. It will certainly be a birthday that she never forgets.

Most of our tours to Britain have concluded in London. Each person who travelled with me will have special memories of being there, whether it be visits to places like Greenwich, the Tower of London, one of the great cathedrals or to the Houses of Parliament. We are always able to include a really good performance in the West End.

Some of the simple places we have visited are also among the most memorable. Dickens House at 48 Doughty Street is one of those. Another favourite place is Dr Johnson's house in Gough Square, just off Fleet Street. I like to stop at the Cheshire Cheese, just at the entrance to Gough Square, and have a lunch of one of their delicious pies washed down with a good English ale.

On the last day of one of our tours I arranged for our group to visit the old legal district of London. We came past the Inns of Court—the places where barristers have met for centuries. Nearby is the Old Bailey, perhaps the world's best known criminal court. Among the Inns of Court is a chapel where there was a tradition of ringing the bell when one of the legal fraternity died. It was common on such occasions for legal chambers to send a clerk to find out who had died. John Donne, who had once belonged to the Lincoln Inn of Court, knew that 'no man is an island' and that 'any man's death diminishes me'. 'Send not to know for whom the bell tolls,' he wrote, 'the bell tolls for thee.'

I had written as a friend to John Mortimer, the creator of Rumpole of the Bailey, and told him that I was bringing a group to London at that time. He told me the location of the wine bar which, in his books, he describes as Pomeroy's Bar. We arranged to conclude our morning tour of the legal district there and when the group arrived, they found John Mortimer sitting, Rumpole-like, wine glass in hand. Over lunch of steak and kidney pie with a glass or two of Pomeroy's plonk, John told us something of his own life and experiences as a barrister that developed into the life of Rumpole. It was a typically generous gesture and a truly great experience for us. But then it was just one of a multitude of ways in which, for me, Britain *is* great.

CHAPTER 4

ICH SPRECHE DEUTSCH

I STARTED LEARNING GERMAN at school. That puzzling word order, the verbs with so many variations, and then gender—I thought it very odd that the word for girl, 'das Mädchen', is neuter, particularly when I didn't feel neuter. I'll never forget the misery suffered when I tried to write a letter to a prefect I admired, in the language we were both learning. Naturally at age twelve my vocabulary was not great, so the dictionary was called upon for help. 'Dear Tessa' I wanted to start with, and then laboured through a few expressions. There was no response from her, but dismay on my part when I discovered that I had started the letter 'Expensive Tessa'. The dictionary gave alternatives for 'dear'—'liebe' and 'teuere'—and I thought the latter was more euphonious!

It may be an exaggeration to claim that I speak German, however what I learned at school, and developed at university, has been very useful in my travels, not only in Germany but sometimes in other parts of the world as well. In this chapter I want to write about our travels in Austria, Germany and parts of Switzerland, and one of the things people in those lands have in common is that they can say 'Ich spreche Deutsch'.

The three countries have many other things in common in addition to their language. Music is certainly one. Not only have they produced many of the world's great composers and performing musicians, but their inhabitants have an outstanding knowledge and love of music. As well as the similarities there are also many differences among the German speaking peoples. We were to discover some of the similarities and differences as we travelled.

'Vienna, city of my dreams', as the song goes, was popularised by the tenor Richard Tauber, who also won us all with 'You are my Heart's Delight' from Lehár's *The Land of Smiles*. It certainly is a lovely city and one of my favourites. Almost everything we associate with Vienna has pleasant connotations—Viennese coffee, Viennese chocolates. Where better to be at New Year than in Vienna? No city in the world has been home to more famous composers—Haydn, Gluck, Mozart, Beethoven, Schubert, Mahler and the Strausses, to name only a few.

And let me assure you that the Danube *is* blue! Viewed from the high Danube Tower or a hillside on a clear sunny day it can be as blue as—well, the Danube! I must admit that mostly it appears a rather murky brown, but there is a certain delight, as Johann Strauss must have discovered, in seeing that the Danube can be blue.

On many of our tours we have started the itinerary in Vienna, which has a good, manageable airport. A few minutes on the coach, across the Danube, and we are in the city and, if travelling direct from Australia, ready to put our feet up. I have mentioned before that we prefer to stay in centrally placed hotels. If you take a map of the city of Vienna, identify where

HOTEL WANDL, OUR FRIENDLY HOTEL IN VIENNA.

the old city wall was—it is now the Ring Road or Ringstrasse—
and find the hub of that circle, that's where our hotel is—the
Hotel Wandl. It could not have been more centrally located in
this gracious and exciting city. And I call it *our* hotel because
we have stayed there so often that it feels like home.

The Hotel Wandl has been run by the same family for more
than 160 years. It is sufficiently old fashioned to make me feel
at home, but modern enough to be pleasantly attractive. The
front entry leads to a quite narrow foyer offering a nice little
sitting area with comfortable red upholstered chairs. Over the
years I have spent relaxed periods there reading the paper or
waiting to leave on a visit. The reception desk is on the other
side and the faces of Frank and Helmut have been there year
after year. They show a slight Viennese reserve for newcomers,

but a warm smile and 'Grüss Gott' for those they know, and there are kisses all around when we arrive with yet another ISP group.

Helga, the manager, is usually in the office behind the desk, but she joins in the hugging when we arrive. What a team! Always able to give help with directions, book us into a restaurant or get tickets for a performance. Never a hiccup with reservations. Never fazed by any situation, Helga was even calm on the morning that she came to us with the news that a woman who had flown to Vienna to join one of our tours had died before arriving at the hotel.

Opposite the reception desk is a small enclosed bar, which was run by a warmly efficient woman called Sissy, the local diminutive for Elizabeth. Many a late night brandy or coffee has been dispensed to us by Sissy.

Then it's up to the bedrooms, five stories of them. I'm sure things must have been very different 160 years ago, but these days the bedrooms have everything one could want, whether large or small. Some of the rooms open out onto the rather grand circular staircase. My favourite rooms are those which face onto the front street, for they also face the Peterskirche. In these rooms you don't sleep before 10 pm and you wake up at 6 am, because the great clock bells of the church toll regularly except between those hours. I love it.

Breakfast at the Wandl was always the traditional fare— croissants, bread rolls, meat paste, cheese, jam and coffee, though you could have orange juice or an egg for extra payment. Only a couple of years ago did they succumb to the expectation of international travellers for a buffet breakfast. But it is still the special ambience of this hotel that makes you know that you are truly in Vienna and not in yet another hotel that you might find anywhere else in the world.

If you walk out of the hotel and go around Peterskirche you will end up at that wonderful central plaza of Vienna, the Graben. There are nice outdoor restaurants where we have sat many times sipping a 'melange'—a coffee related to cappuccino but with lightly whipped cream. One direction takes us to Stefansdom, the great cathedral with Romanesque facade, Gothic tower and baroque altars. In the other direction, past chic coffee houses like Demels and upmarket dress shops, one soon comes to the Hofburg, the palace of the Habsburgs, now housing some lovely museums. There's an understatement!

The many tours which included Vienna had a secret to their success. Anne, John and myself have a friend, Hans Altenhuber, whom we got to know well at the International Adult Education Conference in Sydney in 1988. Hans was the Director General of Education responsible for adult education throughout Austria at that time, but he had just retired when we started taking tours. He and his truly lovely wife, Isabelle, live in Vienna and were able to help us in arranging speakers and many other aspects of the tours. Hans knows the people and places in Austria worth knowing. He stands tall, is highly regarded in the nation, but has the simple touch. On our first tour of Eastern Europe, when Gough joined me for the first time as leader, we began in Vienna and Hans made so many arrangements for us. Hans and Isabelle met us with gifts of distinctively Viennese chocolate for each of our travellers. When we got everyone settled he suggested, 'We should go to the cathedral and light a candle for your safe arrival, and another for the safety and success of your journey ahead.' With a hotel like the

Wandl and friends like Hans and Isabelle, we always felt very comfortable and secure.

We usually started a tour of Vienna by making two circuits of the Ringstrasse in the coach. There is so much to see that you need to go around twice, looking to the left on the first circuit and to the right on the second. Many of the great buildings of Vienna are here—the opera house, the parliament, the university, the town hall, wonderful views of the Hofburg and statues including General Radetzky and a gold-plated Johann Strauss. Sometimes we include a tour of the centre of the city in horse-drawn carriages, and that is a really splendid way to see Vienna. It's a bit of a hike up to the seats behind the coachman, but I wouldn't miss it for anything.

Somehow music seems to dominate so much of the life of Vienna, particularly for visitors. The city officials point out that there are more seats in theatres per head of population than in any other city in the world. We have taken our groups to the Staatsoper, the Volksoper and the majestic Musikverein—it is the one where the internationally televised New Year's concert is held—and other venues like the Hofburg, where we have seen some grand performances. However I don't think I have had as much fun as the times we have been to the Konzerthaus for an evening of waltz and operetta music. The music of Strauss and Lehár dominates these, and they have a very good resident orchestra and talented soloists. I think the Viennese feel that they own this music and they perform with a certain freedom and enjoyment that is quite infectious. Traditionally these concerts never have 'The Blue Danube' or 'The Radetzky March' on the program, but always include them as encores. I have clapped till my hands were sore.

Peter Egan, who leads our music tours, tells me of taking a group to the Staatsoper when the Australian, Simone Young, was conducting the orchestra. At the end of the opera our group of Australians met her at the stage door and presented her with flowers. She greeted the group warmly and spoke to everyone individually. Later, as the group was wandering slowly up the Kartnerstrasse towards the Hotel Wandl, she bounded up from behind and walked with them. It was then they realised that Simone was also staying at the Wandl—'I always stay there,' she explained.

There are many nice restaurants in Vienna, but for a relaxed night out I really enjoy going to a *heuriger* outside the city. This is an eating house attached to a vineyard and cellar where the owner is permitted to sell his own new wine along with food. I have spent many wonderful evenings in that environment. There is inevitably music, always a violin, sometimes an accordion, and the musicians stroll around among the diners. One evening Hans spoke to the violinist and then explained that this man was a Gypsy and his violin was more than 200 years old. 'Would you play us some Gypsy music?' one of the group asked. 'I'll play you one of my own compositions, if you like,' he offered. We were carried away.

The menu in a *heuriger* doesn't offer much choice, but invariably includes schnitzel and strudel. Some of us were talking about the recipe for this Viennese dessert and I was surprised when Hans entered the discussion. 'To make a really good strudel,' he said with a wicked smile, 'as well as flour and apples, you need more than a thousand years of the Catholic Church and six hundred years of the Habsburg Empire.'

THE GYPSY VIOLINIST WOOS ISABELLE.

The Vienna Woods has a special place in everyone's heart because of its musical connections. We could almost hear the music of Johann Strauss as we drove along. Once we stopped for lunch at the Hotel Hölrichmühler where Franz Schubert wrote his song 'The Linden Tree'. The tree which inspired him has gone, but the melody really lingers on. Continuing on through the woods we came to Baden, a colourful resort and spa town where the Viennese love to escape for a holiday. We stood with a sense of joy outside the house where Beethoven had stayed while composing his Ninth Symphony.

Another musical visit I thoroughly recommend is to Eisenstadt, about an hour's drive from Vienna. It was there that Joseph Haydn spent much of his life as musician in the Esterházy Palace. On his tomb are the words and music that he wrote as the national anthem of imperial Austria. After the empire collapsed in 1918 the tune was taken by the Germans for their stirring

'Deutschland, Deutschland, über alles'. At the Esterházy Palace
we enjoyed a wonderful string concert, but found that this particular piece of music was played more as a lament for a lost empire.

The other Austrian city where we have stayed happily on
many occasions is Salzburg. To preserve the historic centre, the
authorities have banned the entry of coaches and other large
vehicles. Given our much stressed preference for centrally
located hotels, it meant a rather difficult arrival as we had to
leave the coach at a parking station outside the centre and take
a smaller vehicle, or walk, to the Hotel Kasererbrau, which is
situated below the convent. A favourite activity for many of our
participants has been to climb the nearby steps to the convent
in the late afternoon and listen to the nuns' singing.

On one of our first tours to Salzburg we chanced on a guide
named Horst who, we learned later, had long been a well-
known music critic. He gave us a marvellously insightful tour
of his city, and at the end of that day we asked whether he
would be prepared to guide and generally look after our future
tours in Salzburg. He has been with us ever since and has been
able to make excellent suggestions for our visits, as well as
making reservations and guiding us. Horst is a tall man—tall
enough for me to look him straight in the eye. When he is not
guiding groups he still writes his critiques. When we first met
him he wore his hair tied back in a ponytail, Mozart fashion.
On later occasions he told me of his matrimonial problems and
then his latest wife made him cut his hair!

It seems that there is no aspect of Salzburg or any of its
musical connections that is beyond the ken of our Horst. He
expects everyone to be as interested in music and Salzburg as
he is. If you're not listening he is likely to have a sharp word

about casting his pearls ... He led us into the city square and the cathedral. Among his interesting facts: 'This is where Gruber, who wrote the music for *Silent Night,* was christened.' He turned on his heel and set off at quite a pace. At last he came to Mozart's house in Getreidegasse. We loved the visit there. He never mentions *The Sound of Music.* Most Austrians don't, unless they have a good commercial reason for doing so.

Salzburg boasts a large number of music halls and theatres, and we have experienced performances in many of them. My favourite for an entertaining evening is to take the funicular to the top of the mountain which dominates the centre of the city. Here is the old fortress where concerts are held regularly, mostly with the music of Mozart and his contemporaries. It is the real essence of Salzburg music.

The history of Salzburg goes back to Roman times when salt from the mines was traded with southern cities. For most of the second millennium it was an independent city state ruled by prince archbishops. In 1816, twenty-five years after the death of Mozart, it was incorporated into Austria. Horst pointed out that Mozart regarded himself as being part of the German Empire, never an Austrian. He went on with a smile: 'But then we have managed to convince the world that Mozart and Beethoven were Austrians, and that Hitler was German.'

A trip around Lake Wolfgang makes an excellent day out. The hills, which I must admit are alive with the sound of music, lead up to the snow-covered alps. Horst took us along the southern side of the lake to Bad Ischl—another spa town as the prefix 'Bad' implies. It was a favourite watering place of the Austrian emperors. We called at the church where Anton Bruckner had at one time been the organist. We walked on to the Zauner pastry shop, which produces goods renowned all over Europe. Naturally we stopped for coffee and cake.

By lunchtime we had come along the northern shore to the town of St Wolfgang. The church here is visited by pilgrims, but we had a different priority and were looking forward to visiting its most famous hotel, The White Horse Inn. We were booked in for lunch in the dining room which looks out over the lake. The White Horse Inn was the setting for the well-known operetta of the same name. It's the usual story of boy meets girl, boy loses girl, but in this case the emperor turns up and sorts out the problem so that they live happily ever after. The music is very catchy and on one of the tours we were delighted with a performance of *The White Horse Inn* at the Volksoper in Vienna, just a day or so after lunching at the Inn.

At the end of the film version of *The Sound of Music* there is a scene where the Von Trapp family is seen heading up a hill to walk into Switzerland. The few residents of Salzburg who have seen the film are keen to point out that if the Von Trapps had walked up that particular hill, they would have walked straight into Germany. Certainly we went on to Germany, but by a much easier route.

Germany's main international airport is at Frankfurt am Main—the place where we have also started tours. Frankfurt is the hub of the very efficient railway network, as well as being an important cultural city. For centuries the various kings and princes who comprised the Electors of the Emperor of the Holy Roman or German Empire met in Frankfurt for the election. In the eighteenth and nineteenth centuries it was the seat of the German parliament.

These days Frankfurt is the main financial city of Germany—perhaps of Europe. We stayed in one of the newer hotels, which serves the financial community. It was neat, smart, comfortable and very efficient. At breakfast one of our group ordered eggs, in German, from the egg cook (all good buffets boast such a person). He looked at us blankly and said that he was Irish and didn't speak German. He went on to explain that in the financial heart of Frankfurt, English is the lingua franca.

Not far from our hotel was the Stock Exchange, and we went there one evening to have dinner in the cellar below it. It's a building which holds pride of place in the city. A larger than life bronze bear and bull adorn the pavement outside, symbols of hope or apprehension to those entering.

Despite its past and present importance, Frankfurt is not a large city—it's considerably smaller than Adelaide. In fact, to draw comparisons with Australia, there is not a city in any of the German speaking countries which is as large as Sydney.

One of the visits which I particularly enjoyed in Frankfurt was to the Goethe House Museum. Johann Wolfgang von Goethe was born in Frankfurt and is usually identified as a poet and dramatist, but we were reminded on our visit that he was a many-sided genius who also made significant contributions to mathematics, biology, architecture, politics and philosophy. His poems are best known as songs, set to music by Beethoven and Schubert. His life was complicated by many love affairs and it is claimed that his sense of guilt over one of these inspired his most famous literary work, *Faust*. The story of Faust selling his soul to the devil is best known to us through the opera by the French composer Gounod, and I thought of times I had seen it performed, none better that in the Bolshoi theatre in Moscow some time earlier.

It is not far from Frankfurt to the Rhine, where we stayed on the banks of the river in the deluxe and romantic Hotel Krone Assmannshausen. It had been established in 1541 and boasts of having had Richard Strauss and Herbert von Karajan as guests. We looked across the river to hillsides covered with vineyards. There are castles, castles everywhere, and picturesque little riverside towns. At night the castle directly across the river from us was floodlit—it would take a lot to beat it for atmosphere. There are train lines on both sides of the river and one insomniac in our group counted more than eighty trains passing in just one night, but I must admit that, being rather exhausted from the long haul from Sydney, I slept soundly.

Not far from our hotel was the convent established by Hildegard of Bingen in the twelfth century, and it is still a very active community. I was familiar with the chants that she wrote and find them to be most beautiful religious music, but I had not realised that her writings on natural history and medicine are regarded as pioneering works on these subjects—she was the first to clinically describe migraine, for instance. Hildegard corresponded with Bernard of Clairvaux and they didn't always see eye to eye—I suspect that the charismatic but gentle Bernard found Hildegard rather forceful. We listened to the nuns singing in the chapel and I bought a CD as an ongoing reminder of their harmony.

The following morning we set out for a river cruise on a vessel called *Marksburg*. It was a walk of several hundred metres along the bank of the river from the hotel to the pier, and I was finding the going a little hard with my disobedient hips. Thank God a friendly driver stopped and invited me to take a ride in the front of his truck. I arrived at the pier to the mirth of my fellow and faster walking travellers, who seemed to think it funny that I would be 'riding shotgun' on a truck-load of beer.

'Yesterday the Rhine, today the Mosel,' I wrote in my diary. It is a much smaller and prettier river. Not as many castles as on the Rhine, but we did visit one at Eltz before continuing on our scenic way to the picturesque riverside town of Bernkastel for a wine-tasting—five good whites.

It was intended that I would lead this tour of Germany, but some months before it was due to begin I had trouble yet again with my hip, so Gough offered to assist me on the tour, and if necessary take over the leadership should my health dictate. He could not understand why we were not staying at Hanover—well, you can't stay everywhere. We had planned to pass through there, but not stay. Didn't we realise, said Gough, that Hanover is enormously important as an economic centre in northern Germany and that it had the most famous and beautiful seven-teenth century gardens—surely at the top of the list of 'must see' for our lot? There was disappointment expressed on my co-leader's part that we would only have a short visit, but as we neared the city and realised that we would have a *very* short visit—I copped the lot. With a complicated detour to the closest car park to the Herrenhausen Gardens we were able to recover part of our loss. It was not easy in several senses—it was late, it was a bit of a walk to the nearest entrance and some parts were not free. Most of us settled for glimpses of the four separate and quite different gardens which are linked by an avenue of lime trees. A black mark for me, still not entirely forgiven!

We did, however, stay in Hamburg, Germany's second largest city with a population about half as big as Melbourne.

Hamburg is said to be the city where most Germans would like to live and it is easy to see why. With Lake Alster and the Elbe at its centre, nearly 50 per cent of the city area consists of water, woodlands, parks and gardens. Most German cities have significant art museums, and Hamburg is no exception. The opera performance of Verdi's *Macbeth* which we saw at the Hamburg Staatsoper was extraordinary. An important part of the scenario was the regular appearance of a large group of witches, dressed grotesquely in body stockings with balloons bulging from their bottoms and boobs. I must admit that I found it fun, though I doubted that it should have been fun, and was not surprised when the artistic team was soundly booed at the end.

We had a day trip to Lübeck, one of the original Hanseatic League ports. It's a fascinating place with high gabled houses, massive gates and seven towering steeples. We were fortunate to hear an organ recital in the Marienkirche. According to legend, Lübeckers riding out a long siege ran out of flour and started to grind almonds to make bread, as a result of which Lübeck is now the marzipan capital of the world. We all loved the Niederegger marzipan shop—it is enormous and colourful, rather like a Christmas gift or toy shop—and I let my head go a little.

As I look back through my diary I realise how much I wrote about food. There were big breakfasts, wonderful picnics, hearty dinners—lots of sausage, potatoes, beer and wine. One of the dishes was served with Frau Goethe's Sauce, a rich topping made with plums. In the north we were often given a delicious mixture of red summer berries for dessert. Believing that one should try the regional foods, I ordered the Labskaus, or sailor's dish, for lunch at Lübeck. It really was too much.

A great piece of herring, a pile of lightly cooked spicy beef mince with beetroot and onion rings, and two eggs on top! Pretty grisly—in fact not really to be recommended—but the beer was good.

On the coach to Berlin, Gough spent an hour or so summarising the history of northern Germany. The dynastic families, which had intermarried with those of Britain, Russia and Scandinavia, formed the basis of his talk. Some of the group, at least those who had not travelled with us before, were surprised that he could give such a detailed summary of historical events without the aid of notes.

Berlin had changed dramatically since our previous visit just after the wall came down. A strange legacy of the wall was a wide band of no-man's land where it had stood. It was now filled with cranes in what must be one of the largest building sites imaginable. There were plans to move the German parliament there to make up for the years of destruction in a divided city. We were most impressed by the developments taking place.

One of the recently completed buildings is the Chamber Music Philharmonia Hall, a beautiful pale timber space in the round. We were delighted with a Schubert concert presented by the Chamber Orchestra of Europe conducted by Claudio Abbado—a top orchestra with a top conductor. It was a real treat, with the added participation of mezzo soprano Anne Sophie von Otter—tall, blonde, slim and in great voice.

The grand Pergamon Museum is in the part of the city which was East Berlin, so reunification has meant that it is now easy to visit there. The Altar of Zeus at Pergamon, on the west coast of modern Turkey, was already 2400 years old, but in ruins, when a German civil engineer named Carl Humann obtained permission to excavate and ship them to Berlin in the nineteenth century. They have been reconstructed into a mind-boggling display of the altar within the temple which housed it—a building about seven metres high and over twenty metres long. This in turn is housed in the museum. The Pergamon Museum is a must for anyone interested in history. Certainly all our participants appreciated that.

Reunification has also meant that it is now easy to visit Potsdam. Our first visit there was to the Cecilienhof, an English Tudor style palace where, at the end of World War II, meetings between the Allied leaders determined the division of Europe.

After lunch we visited Sans Souci, the favourite hideaway of Frederick the Great. There is so much to enjoy in the extensive grounds. This was a favourite place for Jim and Elsie, a couple who only twelve months earlier had visited Germany as independent travellers. They told us that they had had no intention of returning so quickly but liked the idea of returning with the Whitlams. Jim and Elsie commented that it was a particular thrill to stand again in the room where Bach had played for Frederick the Great.

Our excellent young guide, Heike, was full of wonderful Fred the Great stories. We were amused by the quote 'To God in Spanish, to women Italian, to men French and to my horse *Ich spreche Deutsch!*[*]

There was a poignant but unforgettable moment on the way to Potsdam. Hetty and Egon, who were travelling with us, had both fled Germany before the war. They met in Australia where they married. They had been on other ISP tours and sought the emotional security of our group to return to the land of their birth. Hetty had grown up in Berlin and she particularly wanted to see her former home. She remembered the locality and we offered to go through that neighbourhood so that she could find the house. It turned out to be in a street so narrow that it was not possible to take the coach along it. We suggested that Hetty walk along the street and the coach would pick her up at the other end. Almost the entire coach load of travellers jumped off to walk with her and to support her in her pilgrimage. To her amazement there were few changes to the street, except that her home, and hers alone, had been destroyed by bombing. She had long felt a desire to return there, and she told us how much she appreciated us walking with her.

Hetty was also able to find an old friend whom we gladly invited to join us. The friend told us how her husband had been killed on the Russian front. When the Red Army approached Berlin she fled into the forest with her two daughters, living on berries until the situation settled down. This woman was not herself Jewish, but had helped some who were to escape. Hetty's mother had been grateful for her help in leaving Germany in 1938.

We were reminded in Berlin of the vagaries of the German language. When John F Kennedy made a grand speech on his visit to the city in 1963, he wanted to identify with the locals. 'Ich bin ein Berliner,' he announced, much to the hilarity of his audience. To say that he was a person of Berlin he should have said simply, 'Ich bin Berliner.' *Ein Berliner* is the name given in Germany to a doughnut.

NAPOLEON STAYED HERE.

Our journey around Germany took us next to Saxony. On earlier tours we had found it difficult to get suitable accommodation in Dresden, the main city, so we arranged to stay in the Hotel Deutsches Haus, in the nearby town of Pirna. The town and the hotel exceeded our expectations—lovely and history filled. A sign to one side of the hotel indicated that Napoleon had stayed there for ten days in 1813. We stayed for only three.

The journey to Pirna from Berlin was both interesting and eventful. I was fascinated first by the new Mercedes coach which took us on this leg of the journey. A very confident driver was proud of the navigation device on which he would be relying for the trip. He had set the destination to Pirna, and assured us that it would show him the way. Each time he came to an intersection the roads would appear on the screen and an arrow showed him which one to take. As we travelled down the main road he suddenly turned off onto a side road, explaining that there was some obstruction on the road and it had shown him how to make a diversion.

We arrived safely in Pirna. It is not a large town, but somehow our driver's navigation machine could not get him to the hotel. Of course, with a machine like that he hadn't bothered to bring any maps. For forty-five minutes we drove round and round Pirna taking directions from the locals. Give me a map any day, I thought to myself.

A highlight of the trip this day was a stop at Wittenberg, Martin Luther's town and cradle of the Reformation. The doors of the Castle Church, where Luther nailed his ninety-five theses in 1517, have been replaced with bronze ones. That certainly discourages anyone else from nailing theses there! The current bronze doors have Luther's words imprinted on them. Beside the church is the castle, which inspired Luther's most famous hymn. On its tower is written the first line 'Eine feste Burg ist unser Gott'—best known to us as 'A mighty fortress is our God'.

We had lunch in Wittenberg, some having the specialty of the café, and probably the region—potato cakes with smoked salmon and salad. As we left the city the women in our group were chuckling over a strange experience at the town's public toilet, where they had each paid a Deutschmark to the male attendant for the privilege of using it. After about a minute the attendant walked along the corridor blowing a whistle and calling out that it was time to leave.

We drove through Leipzig where, for me, the strongest association is with Johann Sebastian Bach, perhaps the greatest of composers. What a tremendous figure in the development of music and what a heritage of music he left. The second half of his life was spent as organist and director of the choir school at St Thomas Church here. In the following century Richard Wagner was born in Leipzig and attended St Thomas choir school. Gough was more keen to see the great memorial outside the city to commemorate the Battle of the Nations of 1813. This had been a defeat for Napoleon and a turning point in his territorial and imperial ambitions. We passed by Colditz Castle, used during World War II as a prison for Allied soldiers who had a propensity for escaping. We reminded one another of our favourite scenes from the film based on the castle in that era.

I was pleased to note the improvements in Dresden since our previous visit, which had been just after reunification. There are still many buildings waiting to be restored, but the city is coming very much to life. The nearby town of Meissen, famous for its ceramics factory, was not bombed but years of neglect after the war showed their effects.

The highlight of Dresden, however, was a performance we saw of the opera *Tannhäuser* at the Semperoper, where it had first been performed. Eva Johansen played a glorious Elizabeth, but there was a terrible Tannhäuser—a greasy blond chap with no style and a not so marvellous voice. The opera is one of Wagner's earlier successful works and was written in Dresden while he was conductor of the opera.

The Semper Oper has been restored to its former glory, and it really is glorious. Jim and Elsie told me that that evening at the Semperoper was a tour highlight for them. 'It was magic to step out onto the balcony at the interval, sip sekt and take in the moonlit Zwinger, the cathedral and the old bridge over the Elbe.' As we left that night we all gasped at the beauty of the view back across the lake to the floodlit opera house. For us all it will stay as a permanent and charming memory.

Wagner would also stay with us, in a manner of speaking, for much of the rest of our travels in the German speaking countries. We were certainly aware of him when we stopped at Beyreuth. We had time to visit Wahnfried, Wagner's former home and now a museum revealing much of the town's history. We saw the theatre built specially to perform his operas, especially the Ring Cycle.

The south of Germany, particularly the Rhineland and Bavaria, is the part of the country most visited by tourists, and this fact is reflected in the price of hotels, restaurants and most other things that tourists use. The great beer halls with their oom-pa-pa music are enjoyed by the Bavarians as well as many tourists, and I must admit having spent some happy nights in their boisterous surroundings. However the highlight of Munich for me on this visit was to spend several hours in the Pinakothek, the art museum, with a most helpful guide named Erika. I particularly loved the collection of early European paintings.

Our visit took place during the lead-up to the Olympics, Sydney 2000, so we were keen to see the site of the 1972 Games which had been held in Munich. We saw how much the Olympics had affected the city, particularly in the provision of facilities which have been used to great benefit since. The Munich Olympic village was built to house 5000 athletes but is now a residential area for 12000 people. Of course the number of athletes participating increases with each Games, and we realised how the heritage of facilities in Sydney will be significant for many years to come.

THE GARDEN AT ST REMY DE PROVENCE WHERE VAN GOGH WAS HOSPITALISED.

If this isn't fairyland, tell me what it is? A night view from our window in the Hotel Rossiya, Moscow.

Wordsworth loved Rydal Mount—so did we.

Playing games in a heuriger, just outside Vienna.

Always room for a little more. Thank you, Mamma, Castello di Volpara, Tuscany.

CAN IT BE TRUE? THE VIEW FROM MY WINDOW IN ASSISI.

FROM THE BALCONY OF THE HONEYMOONERS' SUITE AT POSITANO.

THE MINOAN PALACE AT KNOSSOS WITH TYPICAL DOLPHIN DECORATIONS.

A TUSCAN TREAT FOR THE EYE.

ANNE AND I IN A GIRLISH MOOD WITH ORCHIDS, IN THAILAND.

PRETTY BUILDINGS AND PRETTY PICTURES FOR SALE, BUENOS AIRES.

WITH MY FAVOURITE MAN, WHERE ELSE BUT AT THE MONUMENT OF LOVE IN LIMA?

PICKET FENCES, PAINTED HOUSES AND CHILDREN—IN SIBERIA.

THE BEST OF GROUPS—ISP NATURALLY—IN THE BEST OF PLACES, THE DEVIL'S THROAT, IGUAZÚ.

Travelling south through Bavaria towards the alps we passed those romantic nineteenth-century castles built by Ludwig II, King of Bavaria, just before he was certified insane. Neuschwanstein is the one that was copied for Disneyland. Most of our group climbed the steps to its neighbour, Hohen-schwangau, while Anne and I prepared a picnic beside the Blue Lake. It was a beautiful day and this is really beautiful countryside. The castle made a wonderful backdrop for an idyllic lunch spot.

As we were preparing the food a crabby Englishwoman came and sat down in the middle of the bench we were using as a table. We suggested that she might be kind enough to move to another seat—there were others available nearby. 'No, I want to sit here,' she muttered. You meet all sorts travelling! She doesn't know how lucky she was not to get a drink down her back as we clambered around her eating our lunch. As we finished our lunch she stood up, produced a camera and, to my amazement, asked if someone would take her photo for her. One of our men volunteered. She posed on the edge of the lake with the castle in the background. 'Say cheese,' the co-opted photographer called as he pointed the camera at the sky and pressed the button. No doubt she was greatly surprised when she got her film developed. The silly old fool!

The Black Forest is another of those localities in the south much favoured by tourists. I particularly love the variations on alpine chalets that are unique to this area—the traditional houses made of timber which has been darkened over time, and set among the deep green trees. They are indeed beautiful. I am not so sure that they would be easy and warm to live in. A walk through the Black Forest to see a waterfall was on the program for the more active in our group. I joined those who just wanted to enjoy the folk museum, the shops with cuckoo clocks, and sitting in the sun with a good coffee.

Germany, Austria and Switzerland meet around Lake Constance. We stayed for several days in the delightful German town of Lindau beside the lake. The Swiss alps, where the Rhine rises before flowing into and out of Lake Constance, can be seen on the other side. We travelled a few miles to hear a superb concert of Mozart and Tchaikovsky music in the Hall of the Knights at Hohenems, on the Austrian side of the lake.

I am quite fascinated by the subtle language and person-ality differences between the people in this part of Switzerland and their neighbours in Germany and Austria. Switzerland has no mineral resources, learning instead to rely on its human resources and to take full advantage of its delightful country-side. Work, save and establish your own home are strong ethics in each of these countries, but nowhere are they stronger than in Switzerland. I've written quite a bit about food as we've travelled through these countries and there are national and regional differences in both food and language. One of the differences I have noted is that while potatoes are common to all the cuisines, in Germany they are known as *kartoffel,* in Austria as *erdäpfel,* in Switzerland as *härdöpfel* and in western regions as *grundbira.*

Crossing borders between Austria, Germany and Switzer-land these days is barely a formality. Usually the border guard checks with the driver or tour leader to ascertain where the group is from. 'Australia'—we are waved through. But this was not always the situation. On our earlier tours the guard would walk through the bus checking each passport, and sometimes we would all have to get off the bus and file past an officer at the desk. On one such occasion coming from Germany into Switzerland we got off the bus, filed past the desk, got back on the bus and took off. Some minutes later we realised we were missing one woman. We turned the bus around and headed back, only to discover that there was nowhere the bus could do a U-turn at the border post. The only option was to re-enter Switzerland, then re-enter Germany—this time *with* the woman who had whipped into the loo on our first stop.

We have taken a number of tours into Switzerland, but have always stayed in the German speaking northern part of the country. The best memory I have of Zurich was of the night several years ago when we took a group to a performance of Rossini's *La Cenerentola* at their excellent opera house. It is the story we know as Cinderella, but Rossini replaces beauty and magic as the primary elements with respect, love and intrigue. On the way to the theatre I suggested to the group that they take particular note of the soprano playing Cinderella, Cecelia Bartoli, as her star was rising in the operatic world. The years since have brought her to full radiance.

My favourite city in Switzerland is Lucerne, so you will not be surprised to know that it is where we usually stay. The city is at the end of Lake Lucerne where it forms into a river. The Kappellbrücke, the covered bridge that crosses the river near this junction, is the most recognisable landmark of the city, and one of the most recognisable in the whole of Switzerland. We have stayed in a hotel on the right bank where most of the rooms look out at the Kappellbrücke—it really is a most delightful place to be. The bridge has been there since the fourteenth century, though I suspect most parts have been replaced many times. When it burned down a few years ago it was replaced within twelve months, looking exactly the same as it always had, dripping geraniums its full length.

I feel comfortable and at home in Lucerne. Parts of the old medieval wall still stand with their watchtowers at intervals along it. As each hour approaches the bells from a dozen churches and public buildings start to chime.

There are also some excellent restaurants which serve the specialties of the alps. Great food if you enjoy sausages, fondues and beer, not so good if your dietary requirements don't match theirs. We had a vegetarian with us on one of the early tours. Their best effort at a vegetarian meal was a plate of carrots. I think—well, I hope—that things have improved in recent years!

I did say that Wagner would stay with us on our travels in the German speaking countries. We found that he was in Lucerne, too. While he was the conductor of the opera in Dresden in the mid nineteenth century, he became involved in a revolutionary movement and was exiled from Saxony. He found refuge for the next thirteen years in Lucerne. His house, Triebchen, set in a park looking over the lake, is where he wrote the operas of the Ring Cycle. It is now a museum which our groups have really enjoyed visiting.

Tradition has it that the legendary William Tell lived by this lake while he was a champion in the fight for independence from the Austrians. He is remembered for his archery skills, but mostly because Schiller and Rossini immortalised him in music. *Wilhelm Tell* is the name of one of the boats which ply around the lake conveying mainly tourists and school children. We often take the boat one way between Lucerne and Vitznau and drive the other. We then enjoy the track rail to Mt Rigi, from

THE TOP OF MT RIGI IS AS CLOSE TO HEAVEN AS YOU GET.

which there are spectacular views of the green countryside, the neighbouring mountains and the lake. There is something wonderful about being on the top of a mountain in the alps—a sense of wonder, even euphoria as you feel that you are on top of the world. If the mist foils us in seeing the view then there's always a hot chocolate to compensate!

On many of our tours we came back to Vienna to conclude the itinerary. One time I talked to Hans about the interesting differences in the way German is spoken, and the differences between the German and Austrian people. We talked about the Austrian traditional greeting *Grüss Gott* (literally 'Greeting God') rather than *Guten Morgen*. Then there is the personal *Servus* in leaving, rather than *Auf Wiedersehen*. 'It is from the Latin mass,' Hans explained. 'It means, but not in a demeaning way, "I am your servant".'

'It's true that we speak the same language as the Germans, although there are differences,' Hans said, 'but we are really very different people.' Waving his hands and smiling, he summed it up as: 'If there was a problem, a German person would look at it and probably say "the situation is serious, but not hopeless". An Austrian would look at the same problem and say "the situation is hopeless, but not serious".'

---

*Actually, those words were used by Emperor Charles V over 200 years earlier. Frederick the Great is remembered for saying, 'My people and I have come to an agreement which satisfies us both. They are to say what they please and I am to do what I please'.

INTERLUDES IN ITALY

PERHAPS THE MOST DRAMATIC way to enter Italy is over an alpine pass, and that was the way we came on one of our first ISP tours. It was a lovely day as we left Switzerland and headed for Italy, so our driver suggested that he take us over the old St Gotthard Pass rather than using the short cut through the tunnel. By the time we reached the summit it was cold and bleak with snow lying about—just the way an alpine pass should be. We went into the chalet at the top, which is there to meet the needs of travellers, and ordered hot chocolate. I love it, but never more than on a day like this in the alps. While we were enjoying our hot drinks the door opened to admit a blast of cold air and two monks in habits. One of my group suggested that they may have left their St Bernard dogs outside—I laughed, but it did fit the location. However, we were soon descending the Italian side of the alps. The sheer limestone cliffs gave way to orchards where apples, pears and peaches were ripening, and grapes and olives were almost ready for harvest. The tranquil Italian lakes of Maggiore, Lugano and then Como came into view. What a romantic way to enter Italy. But then I have always found interludes in Italy to be romantic.

My mind went back thirty-four years to the time I first went to Europe, and that visit of course included Italy. I was as excited as a ten year old. We visited Rome, Florence and Venice, and had experiences such as an audience with the Pope and lunch with Tito Gobbi at his villa. I discovered then that a tour includes the expected and the unexpected—especially in Italy—and I commenced what was to become an addiction: keeping a record of the people, places and provisions enjoyed on my travels. On our ISP tours I was not able to repeat all the experiences I'd previously enjoyed but they did influence our programs and itineraries.

On this tour we planned, as usual, to spend a reasonable amount of time—three or four days—in each of several regions within the country. That way you have time to get the feel of a city or region. Most people start a tour of Italy in Rome, so I will start there too.

You could spend many days in Rome and still not see all the well-known places. Despite that, a brief city tour can provide a good overall picture, and that is what we did on arrival with our first ISP group. Our guide Velia ('Rhymes with Australia,' she pointed out), a chirpy little lady with net stockings and a carnival-coloured walking stick, took us first to St Peter's and the palace entry with its colourful guards. Then we drove along the grand streets and boulevards, through the Borghese Gardens, and along some narrower back streets as well. We were getting a feel for the place—the Colosseum, the Pantheon, the Spanish Steps and finally the Trevi Fountain, where scores were sitting in the sun, some throwing the traditional coins into the water. When we got back to the hotel I noted in my diary: 'Now absolutely pooped but Rome has taken on a new perspective for me'.

Rome is very different to any other city in the world. *La Città Eterna*—the Eternal City—was founded in 753 BC and it has been claimed that during the height of the Roman Empire it was home to the greatest number of magnificent buildings ever to be in one place. Only a few buildings survive from that period because a thousand years of neglect and devastation followed the fall of the Roman Empire, and the city was almost deserted. The Colosseum is the largest and most dramatic building from this era and we explored it with fascination. Some of us were most interested in discovering where the lions and Christians would have fought. On the other hand Ross, one of our engineers, was busy examining the structure: 'It's amazing that a freestanding multistorey theatre, with its arch construction, could be so well built that it survived 2000 years of weather and human destruction,' he pointed out to us.

During the Renaissance there was a renewal of the city with some wonderful buildings, paintings and sculptures by Michelangelo. St Peter's is one of the buildings from that period, though it was not completed till centuries later. Rome has been the capital of a united Italy since 1871, and most of its streets and buildings were constructed in the nineteenth and twentieth centuries. One of our travellers noted that its population was actually not as large as Sydney's.

Over the next few days we had time for longer visits to some of the must-see places. We had two hours at the Vatican museum, where Velia came into her own as a guide. She knew all the treasures—every sculpture, tapestry and painting. I was interested to see a self-portrait of Raphael—a very pretty boy—in the corner of one of his grand pieces. The Sistine Chapel was, as always, the highlight of the museums. Many claim that the ceiling by Michelangelo is the world's greatest art work, and I have no reason to disagree with that.

I do like Italian food and particularly enjoyed having dinner in the Piazza Navona one evening. Fountains (two of them by Bernini) make the Piazza Navona one of the more pleasant places in Rome to visit and to dine, although it can get rather crowded in the tourist season. We were outside on a coolish evening, but we were well covered by those big Italian market umbrellas. The menu: antipasto, pasta (spaghetti all'amatriciana and fettuccine con funghi porcini), arrosto di vitello con patate, insalata mista, with very rich tiramisu to follow and, of course, wines and coffee.

We were in Rome during the opera season. It does not run for long and it is not easy to get tickets, but we were fortunate. We saw an excellently sung performance of Bellini's *La Sonnambula*. Amina was superb, the tenor and bass also splendid. In Italy, however, every singer must please the audience all the time, and some of the locals occasionally voiced their disapproval with a few boos.

Before leaving Rome I was glad to have the opportunity of visiting the Villa Adriana and nearby Tívoli to see the Villa d'Este. The Villa Adriana dates from the second century AD Emperor Hadrian who, although he was Spanish, was inspired by Greek architecture. It is set in enormous grounds but we successfully found a good corner of the ruins where I most enjoyed the varied black and white mosaic floors of Hadrian's *Hospitalia* or guest house.

Villa d'Este, which is most renowned for its landscaped gardens, was constructed in Renaissance times. The gardens make good use of stone walls and fountains, and would bring delight to any garden lover, old time or modern. Judging by the crowds in Rome and the few who were at these estates, most visitors miss out on these treasures.

I find Rome to be an amazing, awe-inspiring and alluring city. I must admit that on that last sunny day during our visit I, too, threw a coin into the Trevi Fountain in the hope that I would return yet again.

The road south from Rome to Naples is broad and straight and runs through flat and fertile farmlands. The appearance of Mt Vesuvius afforded us some preparation for the country immediately to the south, where rugged mountains and narrow winding roads bring us to the spectacular Amalfi coast. The almost sheer cliffs face south, directly to the equator and the rarely clouded sun. The limestone dissolved in the sea means that the waters at the bottom of the cliffs reflect a rare and beautiful blue. It is regarded by Italians as the most beautiful coast in Italy and I'm sure few places anywhere in the world could lay claim to greater beauty.

Positano, which is tucked away in one of the tiny bays along the coast, is built to take the greatest advantage of the cliffs, the sea, the weather and the sheer beauty. We stayed in the Hotel Poseidon, built, as are all the others, in the only place possible—on the side of a cliff. The guest relations manager of the hotel was Jenny, an Australian escapee to this paradise. As soon as I saw our room I was thrilled. Number 32 was a lovely room opening onto a grand terrace, and had sweeping views of the town and the coast. I soon discovered that all were equally delighted with their rooms, which had the same wonderful view. We ate breakfast on the terrace each morning, and in the evenings we would gather there for drinks as the sun set. All was very well with our world.

Travel along the Amalfi coast is something of a nightmare. The road hugs the cliffs about 300 metres above the water's edge—hard enough if you are in a small car with all the traffic going the same way, but it is a two-way road and there are dozens of buses jostling with hundreds of cars. In Positano it is not possible to take a coach into the streets of the township, so minibuses ply their way constantly from the main road, down among the hotels and houses to the tiny town centre by the water, then up the other side to the main road again. When we were first arriving by coach from Rome, Jenny had told us to stop the coach at the angel as we approached Positano on the main road, and the minibuses would bring us the rest of the way. The angel? Sure enough there was a blue concrete angel, such as could only be found in the south of Italy, standing serenely by the road, with sufficient space beside her for us to unload from our coach.

As well as being noted for its beauty and pleasant lifestyle, Positano is well placed for visits to the south of Italy. Huw Evans, who leads garden tours for ISP, has pointed out to me that some of the best gardens in Italy—indeed, some of the most interesting in Europe—are in this region.

There are daily boats from Positano to Capri—which the Italians, unlike American songwriters, accent on the first syllable. We walked down to the marina through lanes of shops, shops and shops with our guide named Guido, who had brought his girlfriend along for the day out with us. As well as pointing out the landmarks he handled the complicated system of boats and buses well on this exceptionally busy island. We passed the entrance to the Blue Grotto, but weren't counting on going in as the tide was high and the tourists too numerous. The Emperor Tiberius and Gracie Fields are among those who have chosen Capri as their home. Our best visit was to the Villa San Michele, former home of Axel Munthe set in exotic gardens at Anacapri, near which I bought a good denim dress for future summer sorties.

In my diary for the following day I wrote 'Pompei' in red ink—then added 'should be writ in red'. In the shadow of Vesuvius, the people of Pompei had no hope of surviving when poisonous gases overwhelmed them at the beginning of an eruption in 79 AD. One of the strange things about the city, as it has been uncovered, is that people appear to have been going about their ordinary activities at the time, and you get such a good idea of the way the city actually worked. The town had some fascinating art—in the house of the Vetti, for instance, with the Priapic fresco near the entrance and in the public baths.

Braving the road along the Amalfi coast was necessary to visit Amalfi and Ravello. We particularly enjoyed visits to the Villa Rufolo, a favourite haunt of Wagner, and the Villa Cimbrone—both have spectacular views. Later, when we stopped at the bottom of a formidable flight of steps leading up to the cathedral in the town of Amalfi, Guido suggested that some might like to climb these to see inside. The group seemed most reluctant to move until Gough announced that he wanted to copy down a Latin inscription he knew of inside and marched up the steps. If he can do it so can I, others thought, and followed his example.

The next region we explored was Umbria. It is a broad valley landlocked within the Apennine Mountains where the Tiber River begins its flow toward Rome. A unique and lovely feature of the area is that most of the traditional towns, like Perúgia, Assisi and Gúbbio, were built on top of hills and rocky outcrops in an otherwise level plane. From a distance they appear to stand like iced buns. Up close we could see the grey stone buildings, each one topped with pipe-like terracotta tiles, clinging to a maze of irregularly shaped streets. Great defence and very picturesque, but difficult to access.

We had arranged to spend four nights in Assisi. Our hotel was the Fontebella, in the Via Fontebella, which unsurprisingly has a beautiful fountain on one side. We had a great view from our room looking over the softly chequerboarded countryside. The higgledy-piggledy houses below us made it look like patchwork fabric.

Our first day in Assisi started with a walking tour of the town. All the houses, offices and shops give the impression of being hundreds of years old. Certainly no newer building is out of style with the ancient ones and repairs and renovations are obviously done with great sympathy for their heritage. In the centre of the old city is the Temple of Minerva which is one of the few, and perhaps the best preserved, temples of Roman times. The dominance of the Basilica of St Francis, and the pilgrim and tourist industry that has been built around this saint, mean that the Temple of Minerva, this architectural gem of classical times, is ignored by the majority of visitors and locals alike.

At the same time it is not possible to visit Assisi without being aware of the presence of St Francis. The humility of the man and his teaching is given the most emphasis. His intense love of nature, and the joy he found in it, inspired his Hymn of Creation, first written in the Umbrian language but translated into many contemporary ones. In reality he was a great negotiator and charismatic leader. After establishing the Order of the Friars Minor he had more than 5000 followers within a decade, and the influence of his Franciscans, as his followers were called, was to spread over much of the old and new worlds. Despite the grandeur of the basilica, which contains some of Giotto's earliest frescos, some of my group told me their favourite was the grotto, in the hills behind the town, where Francis had spent much time alone. It was well depicted in stories we had read as children.

People react differently when we visit a religious site like Assisi. For some it has a deep spiritual significance. Len was one of our travellers who claimed not to be religious, but he suggested that if there was any place in which one might discover the meaning of life, it could be Assisi.

From a distance Perúgia has the same general appearance as Assisi, but it is much larger and has a quite different feeling. It is famous for its international university and its industries, including chocolate making. It is a city almost as old as Rome and, as with most old cities, it has been built and rebuilt many times. I was intrigued to discover that at one stage they had covered over the existing houses and streets and built on top of them, so that there is a subterranean town under the centre of the present one.

One of the quaint things about Perúgia and the other towns of Umbria is that you buy salt at the tobacconists' kiosks. The origin of this practice goes back to the time when Umbria was one of the states which the Pope ruled as monarch. A tax was placed on salt and tobacconists were chosen to distribute the salt and collect the tax. To this day the traditional breads of Umbria are cooked without salt, a habit commenced years ago to avoid the salt tax—I couldn't resist buying a souvenir sack of salt!

We went on to a charming *Museo del Vino* in Torgiano—an immaculate fortified village with great views towards Perúgia. We enjoyed a wine tasting, particularly savouring a lovely white Torre del Giano. I bought two bottles of it to add to that already bought by Anne for the next day's picnic.

As we travelled between Umbria and Tuscany, Gough was giving one of his background talks, this time on the Romans. He'd got to the stage of describing the Punic Wars with Carthage, and how Hannibal had taken his army of 40 000 men and forty elephants through Spain and France, across the alps, and was preparing to attack the Roman legions from the north of Italy. He was just describing how the two armies had met at Lake Trasimeno, and was about to describe the gruesome battle that followed. At that moment we came over a hill and there was Lake Trasimeno right in front of us. Instead of hearing about the battle we stopped for a picnic—hard-crusted Italian rolls, ham, cheese, fresh tomatoes, cornichons and those really good wines.

To explore Tuscany we chose to stay in Siena. During medieval and Renaissance times it had been an independent city–state often at odds with Florence, until the Medicis managed to take control of both cities. We preferred Siena because it is accessible, friendly and knowable as well as being a really lovely city. The Piazza del Campo, in the middle of the

LAKE TRASIMENO PROVIDES A PICNIC SPOT—NEVER MIND THE WEATHER.

city and surrounded by tall and ancient buildings, is one of the
finest town squares in all of Europe. Scenes of the colourful
Palio always come to mind, as does the depiction of it in John
Mortimer's delightful story *Summer's Lease.*

Near our Siena hotel was an old sixteenth-century Medici
fort. The living quarters and weapons storage areas of the fort
were all underground, making it an ideal area now for storing
wine. It has been converted to a cellar, the Enoteca Italiana,
with the greatest collection of wines from the whole country.
In the good care of Anna, hostess at the Enoteca, we had a delicious dinner with a little chamber music aimed at helping the
digestion.

From Siena we explored the hills and villages of Chianti
country, one of the districts within Tuscany. Mario was at the
wheel of the coach and the lovely and bright Donatella was

our guide. Chianti Classico wines are made with four different varieties of grapes, Donatella explained to us. The Castello di Broglio is one of the most famous in the area and, in fact, it was a di Broglio who created the recipe for Chianti Classico. He had been the first prime minister after the unification of Italy in 1871. Creating new wines seemed to me to be a very useful thing for former prime ministers to do.

After visiting villas and vineyards we headed towards Castello di Volpara for lunch. Donatella urged Mario to take a scenic route through a small valley. He did so rather reluctantly and, sure enough, we became trapped trying to turn a sharp and steep bend. Most of us sat quietly by the creek. Those, like me, who tried to help only succeeded in interfering. It was good to have Ross, our engineer, with us and with his help Mario extricated the bus from where it was snared. Thus it was that we arrived an hour and a half late for lunch. The mamma, who was waiting to serve us in a small tower, was naturally named Maria. What a meal! Pasta, of course, and a delicious dish of chicken, pork and beans; lots of Chianti, cake, *vin santo* and espresso. But the experience was much more than the menu. It was also the wonderment of the *castello* in this divine countryside and the special magic of Tuscany.

While in Tuscany we spent two days visiting Florence, the greatest artistic centre of the world. It is so grand that I hesitate to begin writing about it. During the Renaissance, Florence was fortunate to have the Medici family as patrons of the arts, together with the presence of artists like Giotto, Botticelli, Brunelleschi, Donatello and Michelangelo. Here too worked Leonardo da Vinci, the philosopher Dante, the political theorist Machiavelli, the scientist Galileo and the musician

Rossini. The Uffizi Palace, the Duomo and the Ponte Vecchio loom as architectural treasures and, together with the Accademia, house some of the greatest art treasures. The help of a good guide is always essential and Roberto, who showed us around, was certainly one of the best. We started our tour of Florence at the Piazzale Michelangelo, where we could see the whole city in one breathtaking glance. I was pleased to remind my group that it is a sister city to Sydney.

From Tuscany we travelled to the Véneto, that delightful region west of Venice. The people there have a little ditty they tell about themselves:

Veneziani gran signori,
Padovani gran dottori,
Vicenzini magna gatti,
Veronesi tutti matti.

It is true that Venice was noted for its statesmen, and Padua was most famous for the scholars at its university, but I don't really think that the people of Vicenza ate cats, and to say that *all* the people of Verona are mad has to be an exaggeration!

Our early tours to Italy had Verona as our first stop. It is an ancient city built around the virtually complete old Roman arena which is used these days for a summer festival of opera and ballet. Much of the city is medieval, with narrow streets, marketplaces and some lovely churches.

Verona was the home of two rival families immortalised by Shakespeare as the Montagues and Capulets in his play about the world's most famous romantic couple, Romeo and Juliet. In the courtyard of one of the homes of the Capulets a balcony was added some years ago, and a bronze statue of Juliet stands below it. It is right in the centre of the old city and attracts thousands of visitors—as much as we know that the balcony is a recent addition, we still love to stand in the courtyard, charmed by the love story.

The hotel we usually stayed in was the Giulietta e Romeo, right beside the arena and only a few hundred metres from the bustling Piazza delle Erbe. It is a simple hotel with all the enchantment of old Verona. On our first visit we had arranged for porterage for our suitcases to be taken from the coach to the hotel and to our rooms. We had also asked the manager of the hotel to make a reservation for our group for dinner at the restaurant in the hotel—although the restaurant is in the hotel it is run independently. We were to have dinner there on the Sunday we arrived and also on the Monday evening. What happened when we arrived illustrated the carefree—perhaps even a little mad—ways of the locals.

On Sunday afternoon our coach arrived on schedule and parked as near as we could get to the hotel—about three blocks away. Anne went to the hotel, announced our arrival, and asked if the porters could come and collect our bags as arranged and paid for. 'Oh, the porters don't work on Sundays,' said the manager. Anne managed to borrow a trolley from another hotel and for the next half hour the men in the group ferried our bags to the rooms.

Eventually we had the group settled when the manager made the cheerful announcement: 'I've booked your group into the restaurant for dinner tonight and tomorrow night.' We thanked him for doing that. 'By the way,' he added as an afterthought, 'the restaurant doesn't open tomorrow night.'

One of the compensations for the casual ways in which Italians handle things is that in the end they work out all right. On the Monday when the restaurant was to be closed in Verona we had a tour planned to the beautiful and interesting Lake Garda. While Anne and I took the group on a cruise of the lake, John went to a restaurant in Sermione, on the lake's edge. 'Can you feed thirty people in half an hour's time?' John asked the restaurateur. 'Nessun problema,' he replied cheerfully, waving his arms for added effect. John negotiated a price for antipasto, a variety of pastas and main courses, tiramisu and a glass of red wine for each person. Soon we were tucked into a wonderful meal, interrupted only by the fact that it started to rain and some had to move to avoid drips from the ceiling. It was still raining when the food was finished so we had to stay put in the restaurant for an hour or so. The manager kept handing out bottles of red wine and the time passed quickly with appropriate good humour. We were eventually able to leave and John went to settle the account. 'What about the cost of all the extra wine?' John asked after noticing that it was not on the bill. 'Non importa,' the manager brushed off the enquiry.

We have been to some wonderful concerts in Verona, although I now feel some trepidation about taking a group to a performance there. One night we had tickets which showed a concert starting at 8 pm, but when we arrived the notices outside said that it would start at 9 pm. It included local performers and a guest pianist from Russia who played Rachmaninov. It was worth waiting for. On another occasion we arrived at the venue for a private concert, but there were no musicians! About twenty minutes later a noisy and happy group of musicians arrived by bus. On almost every visit here we have arranged for a group of lecturers at the conservatorium to play Renaissance music on instruments of that period—always good value.

Betty was with us on our first tour of Italy. In France she regarded everything as *magnifique*, and soon discovered that here everything was *magnifico*. After a visit in Verona we returned to our bus which was parked in a no parking zone. The policeman standing beside it was about to write nasty things in his notebook. Betty summed up the situation and gave me instructions: 'Quick, lean on me and limp more!' Moments later we were at the door of the bus. 'Oh, officer,' Betty beamed, 'thank you for helping my friend.' Who could resist her smile.

One night we were eating dinner when I became aware of a growing uproar from my group. Everyone was looking to the door where Betty had just entered wearing the most outrageous purple slippers, each shaped like the head of an enormous cat. She had a smile to match. *Tutti matti*—perhaps it *is* catching in Verona.

I always like to visit Vicenza. I must admit that we have not stayed there for a meal, though we were not really put off by those Venetian claims about their culinary preferences. The city is justly famous for its sixteenth-century Palladian buildings. Andrea Palladio introduced neo-classical architecture to Vicenza, from whence it was adopted in other parts of Europe and indeed many parts of the world. The city's centre is dominated by grand white marble buildings of his design. When the German poet Goethe visited Vicenza more than 200 years ago he wrote: 'You have to see these buildings to realise how good they are. [Palladio's] major problem was how to make proper use of columns in domestic architecture since a combination of columns and walls must always be a contradiction. How the

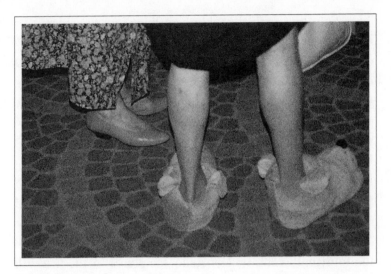

BETTY'S BARGAIN BOOTEES, BACK VIEW.

tangible presence of his creations makes us forget that we are
being hypnotised.'

One of Palladio's last and best works in Vicenza was the
Teatro Olympico, built in the style of a classical theatre. The
whole building is beautiful but it quite amazes me that instead
of a flat backdrop to the stage it has actual houses and streets—
they have real depth, not just a sense of depth. For as long as
I have been visiting Vicenza Mr Rossi, a seemingly always aged
man, has conducted the most delightful and informative tours
of the theatre in English.

My initial fascination with the Véneto increased enormously
after a proper visit to Padua. The propriety of the visit was most
definitely in the Casa dei Pellegrini—the House of the Pilgrims,
a hotel which is right opposite the San Antonio Basilica. Such
a find. Owned by the church and managed by the priests, it has

fantastic rooms with the whitest of linen and the shiniest of marble floors, even in the bathrooms. Cool and clean, its interminable halls make it a refuge in an Indian summer—and maybe a little too cold in winter? A huge restaurant, on the ground floor and across a courtyard, provides plain fare but plenty of it, with lots of wine and water. Luigi runs the restaurant in that wonderful way that makes everyone feel at home. It really is my sort of place.

San Antonio Basilica, an architectural monument to St Anthony of Padua, is impressive more for its content and embellishments than its architectural beauty. Begun in the thirteenth century, it gained frescos by the Giotto school in the fourteenth century, Donatello sculptures in the fifteenth century and many more treasures in the sixteenth and seventeenth centuries, culminating in a Tiepolo in the eighteenth.

Even though I went to a church school for more than seven years, I must admit that I'm not very religious, at least in my observations anyway. St Anthony, however, is a saint of my liking and indeed I still carry a small medallion of the man in his typical pose holding a child. It is said that he helps find things, so some of us in the group keep his likeness close . . .

Padua is very much visited for several special places. My favourite is the Cappella degli Scrovegni, which is easy to find, to visit and to appreciate. It is right by a public garden in the middle of the city and is so tiny that numbers inside are limited, making it difficult for the summer hordes to have time to see all of its fabulous Giotto frescos. It took me three visits to take in the whole plan and to identify, in particular, the vices and virtues depicted on the lower part of either side. Since the chapel was built and donated as a form of penance, it is quite appropriate to turn from folly, inconsistency, wrath, injustice, infidelity, envy and despair to hope, faith, justice, charity, temperance, fortitude and prudence.

Padua is famous for its university, which is the oldest in Italy— one of the oldest in the world, in fact, and has produced great doctors. Shakespeare had Portia appear as a doctor of law from Padua in *The Merchant of Venice*, and certainly its scholars have been renowned for centuries. The university is commingled with offices and shops in the city. The operating theatre in the faculty of medicine has been associated with many advances in medical science, but it is only available for visits by medicos with introductions. On the other hand, the botanic garden attached to the university is equally as old, has been associated with many discoveries in biological sciences, is lovely to behold and open to all.

Padua is a splendid jumping-off place for the whole region, and day trips to Verona, Vicenza and Venice are quite easy. It is also easy to access the lakes and foothills of the alps. Padua is my choice for a holiday in the north of Italy.

One of the nicest ways to arrive in Venice is to travel down the Brenta Canal from Padua. There are quite a number of palaces and villas along the canal which were designed by Palladio or in his style. These can be seen, or at least glimpsed, as you travel in one of the canal boats. The best arrangement is to take, as we did, a full-day boat trip, stopping at several of the villas as well as a enjoying a luxurious lunch at one of the canal-side villages.

One of the grandest of these masterpieces along the Brenta Canal is the Villa Pisani. The interior has rooms around a court-yard in the style of European palaces. Some of the great reception rooms have ceilings painted by Tiepolo. In the extensive and well cared-for gardens a hedge maze kept eighteenth century guests amused—and lost— for hours. It is best seen from a small tower nearby. One of my favourite villas is the Malcontenta, which has the added attraction that the canal boat stops almost at the front door. Unlike Villa Pisani it is quite small, but very charming. The unfortunate name came about because a dissatisfied wife was virtually imprisoned there.

Any way that you arrive in Venice is romantic. Even the trains and the long distance buses come into Piazzale Roma on an outer island, and from there you take a little ferry, or vaporetto as they are called, along a canal to a point near your hotel.

The airport at Venice is across the water from this paradise of islands and on one of our tours we arrived there in the evening. Commencing a tour of Italy in Venice meant a bit of an extended journey from Australia but it was so worthwhile. Paolo, the concierge of our ancient but four star hotel, The Saturnia, made special efforts for us at every turn. Paolo came to the airport to greet us and transferred the entire group plus luggage by three water taxis to a landing near the hotel. The beauty of Venice as we approached it that evening will stay with me forever. Our hotel was only a two-minute walk from the landing, so we quickly settled into our rooms—ours was number 28, overlooking the courtyard and quiet except for the pleasant sound of bells. We had a super dinner of fish risotto, monkfish with spinach and the best, richest zabaglione I've ever tasted.

There followed three days of excellent activities, the first commencing with an early morning gondola ride—six boats for our group—to get the feel of the place and recognise landmarks

THE FOUR OF US ENJOY THE BEST OF EVERYTHING.

like the Rialto Bridge and the Doges Palace. Following that we all walked to the Doges Palace and San Marco Church, with one local guide for the slow walkers (such as me) and another for the supposedly faster. In the ninth century the Venetians brought the relics of Mark, the evangelist, from North Africa to Venice. The relics are in the basilica in the main square of the city. St Mark is their patron saint and the lion, the symbol of Mark, is also the symbol of the city. A feature of the basilica is a wonderful set of mosaics depicting the life and death of the evangelist. I was fascinated with the undulating floor of the church, wondering how much longer grand buildings like this will stand in a city that is gradually sinking.

The *Doge,* or duke, was the elected head of state of Venice. He ruled the city and the region from a palace between St Mark's Basilica and the Grand Canal. The building, one of the main sights, houses a collection of medieval artifacts, some beautiful, others grotesque. Gough and John were fascinated by an early clock, the hands of which moved anticlockwise. In the afternoon we visited the Peggy Guggenheim Gallery, which had been very much 'done up' since Gough and I had visited it years before with Paul Newman, Joanne Woodward and Gore Vidal and shared Peggy's eightieth birthday cake.

Most visitors tend to see Venice as an island divided by canals. The 100 000 permanent residents see it as a group of islands, each a community in its own right and connected to other islands by bridges. It is now something of a living museum for tourists, but I have never met anyone who was not captivated by it.

Certainly there are many things to do in Venice. One of my favourites is to take a boat out to the island of Burano, with a quick stop at Murano and Torcello on the way. These islands lie with Venice in The Lagoon, separated from the Adriatic Sea by the long sand bar or Lido. Murano is noted for its glass-blowers and many colourful pieces are available, at a price, in the attractive glass factories. Best of all is Burano, in many ways like a little Venice, remarkable for its brightly coloured houses, its lace work, calm lifestyle and also for some good eating places. Who can forget the seemingly endless lunch at Romano's with lots of lovely rosé? A sunny day on the islands, including a long lunch, is my idea of bliss.

The Chiesa di Santa Maria Della Pieta is the church identified with Vivaldi. He taught music at the school nearby and much of his music was first performed in the church. We have taken our groups to some memorable Vivaldi concerts there. No matter how chilly it is within the church, the music sends us out glowing.

Among the colonnades of St Mark Square and spilling into the square itself are tables and chairs for hundreds of coffee

On Burano they're all captains.

drinkers. It matters not that one pays about five times as much there as you would in a café in Australia—or in most other parts of the world for that matter. The place is magnetic. I have often sat there sipping coffee and wondering what it is about Venice that attracts the peoples of the world. Certainly the city is grand and reflects the talent of its patrician leadership—the *Veneziani gran signori*. I see the gondolas in the canals around me as they ply their way through the city with their loads of tourists, and remember the times I have travelled in one quite bewitched by this spell. Who knows why? All I know is that Italy is romantic and that Venice epitomises its magic.

CHAPTER

ULYSSES, SOCRATES

AND ST PAUL

I GREW UP AT THE end of an era when a classical education was regarded as essential preparation for a professional life, or indeed for any sort of leadership role. In Australia we followed the British tradition whereby boys, and sometimes girls, were taught the legends of Homer, the philosophy of Plato and details of the Roman Empire—and often to read about them in Greek and Latin. Young men were then sent to manage family enterprises, practise medicine or law, provide good government, lead armies, minister to churches at home or abroad, and to administer colonies. The Old and New Testaments were read at home, at church and at school in the language of sixteenth century England. For many families of my generation, Ulysses, Socrates and St Paul were household names, however it took me some years to accurately associate their names, and particularly the places they frequented, with modern Greece and Turkey.

Gough and I had become familiar with parts of Greece and Turkey during several visits that began more than forty years earlier. With the exception of one lovely week spent travelling down the coast of Turkey, such visits were usually rather rushed. The idea of leading a more relaxed group tour to these two countries appealed to us a great deal. Gough had been raised on the legends of Greece. His father had read them to him as a child, as he had to our own children. At school and university he continued classical studies and has taken a special interest in political and other aspects of modern Greece. He remains the only Australian not of Greek ancestry to have been admitted to the Academy of Athens (1992). In 1996 the Greek government made him a Grand Commander of the Order of Honour and in 1998 awarded him the Grand Cross of the Order of the Phoenix.

We flew to Athens on our first ISP tour to Greece, arriving in the early afternoon. We were met by Eléni, who was to be our guide throughout Greece. On the way to the hotel she took us to Filopappos Hill, one of the main hills of Athens. Directly in front of us was the Acropolis with its crowning masterpiece, the Parthenon. The whole of Athens was spread out, right down to Piraeus, the seaport of ancient and modern times, and we could see out into the Mediterranean. But it was hard to look away from the glory of the Acropolis. If any one site epitomises the epoch that created archetypal standards in great architecture, democratic government and philosophy, it is this. That night I tried to come to grips with the weariness caused by the flight, the reality of being once again in one of the most wonderful cities in the world, and the excitement of three weeks of travel ahead.

As usual John and Anne were with us as managers of the tour, and I was confident that all would flow smoothly. The year following this tour John and Anne were to organise a similar tour with Barry Jones, whom I had approached to succeed the

Whitlams as a leader of study tours. Some of the stories from Barry's tour must be included as we proceed through Greece and Turkey and sail the Greek islands.

In the two tours there was a total of sixty travellers in addition to the leaders. Both had filled quickly with people who had been with us before. Some are already known to you—Alison and Robin (the 'encyclopaedias'), and Father Jim you met first in France; Dr Hugh and Elfie were with us in Russia; you were introduced to Mary the teacher and Charles of Scotland when we journeyed through Britain. I'll tell you about some of their experiences and reactions as we travel. However Betty, the magnificent traveller, was ill and unable to be with us. As I look down the lists now I see that we had some who had different vocations to those I've mentioned before—we had a pharmacist, a college principal, a dentist, a trade union leader, a banker, a singer, a judge, an architect and a biologist. Gough's sister, Freda, who still teaches Latin though she retired from her role as a headmistress years ago, was also with us.

We had seen the Acropolis from Filopappos Hill, but it was now time to climb to the top. Eléni had us make an early start so that we were ahead of the main crowds and the heat of the sun. Athens can get very hot, even before the summer sets in. The area is rather sparse of shade and the white ground and buildings reflect the uninterrupted sun's rays. There is a hard climb to the top which can take twenty minutes with slow-coaches like me. I looked across at Mary, the teacher, who had an inconcealable smile. 'How many times have you taught classes about the Acropolis?' Mary thought for a moment. 'I've lost count,' she replied, 'but I never thought that I would climb it or that it would be as wonderful as this.'

The word 'acropolis' simply means 'a high city'. For defence reasons it was quite common for the Greeks to build an acropolis, and each is referred to as the acropolis of that particular locality. *The* Acropolis is the one in Athens. The main building on top is the Parthenon—the Temple of the Virgin. It was built for the worship of the virgin goddess Athena. Since childhood we had seen it in picture books, text books, on postcards and even on chocolate boxes, but there was no way of comprehending just how huge those columns are, and how enormous the temple is. I have never been with anyone seeing the Parthenon for the first time who was not amazed by its size.

One of the people with Barry Jones at the Acropolis kept asking practical sorts of questions which the guide found rather difficult to handle. 'How many men did they have working on the Parthenon?' 'How did they get water to the top of the Acropolis?' 'Where did people live when the Acropolis was an active community?' Barry later explained to the guide that for many years her persistent questioner had been responsible for the development of Canberra, and that the questions had a very real interest for him. Sir John Overall had, in fact, headed the National Capital Development Commission for fourteen years and more recently been a member of the Parliament House Construction Authority.

We went on to visit the National Archaeological Museum, which is in the centre of the modern city and houses the greatest archaeological treasures of ancient and classical Greece. Eléni's knowledge and communication skills came to the fore as she guided us through this array of statues, gold artifacts, ornaments and frescos. The cases of Mycenaen gold on the ground floor and the frescos from the island of Santorini on the upper floor are my favourites, especially the boxing boys and the boy fishing. Once when Gough was on an official visit to this museum years ago, he embarrassed his hosts by pointing out that one item in the gallery was of the wrong era. I was hoping that he would not interfere on this visit.

The origins of Athens can be traced back about 1500 years BC to the period of ancient Greece, when history and legend are rather mixed—the era of Ulysses. Athens' grand days were in the classical period, starting about 500 BC when democracy was ushered in, the Parthenon was built under the leadership of Pericles, and Socrates, Plato and Aristotle taught in the city. It was still a great city in the Roman period, when St Paul preached in the marketplace about 50 AD.

Athens is also a modern city. It has grand administrative buildings, hotels, churches and commercial buildings—all the trappings of a national capital. The Plaka district is the old market area of the city and most of our travellers tended to migrate there in their free hours. We all loved to walk among the shops and eat in the typically Greek restaurants which serve good Mediterranean food and wine in the open air.

Lord Byron is much remembered in Athens, with statues and parks named in his honour. A delightful little museum in the town hall has a section devoted to him. Some of us had already visited his home at Newstead Abbey near Nottingham. He was a product of a classical education at Harrow and Cambridge and identified strongly with the Greek nationalist movement of the 1820s. 'I dreamed that Greece might still be free', he wrote poetically and hopefully. He was so committed to the cause of rebuilding an independent Greece that he came to assist in the struggle. In 1824 he died during the siege of Missolonghi, on the coast west of Athens, aged thirty-six. He died not in conflict but of fever.

We were reminded that Greece eventually gained independence in 1829 and chose to become a kingdom. They selected a Bavarian prince as the first monarch, but found him to be too autocratic for their liking. When Athens was chosen as the capital it was a small town with a big collection of ruins. It was still small in 1896 and 1900, when it hosted the first two Olympic Games of modern times. In the middle of the twentieth century, when it became a republic, it had a population of a million. Athens has now grown to over three million, though not without pain.

From Athens we set out by coach for a four-day tour through the Peloponnese. This is the large peninsula south of Athens which forms the most southern part of mainland Greece—and, for that matter, mainland Europe. It is the most fertile part of Greece, with groves of olives and citrus trees and extensive vineyards. We all delighted in our travels through it.

It did not take us long to get from Athens to Corinth on the isthmus that joins the Peloponnese to mainland Greece. As the isthmus is only about six kilometres wide at this point, it also forms a link between the Ionian and Aegean Seas, and thus is something of a crossroads. The ancient city of Corinth was extremely important to the Greeks, and later to the Romans, for industry and commerce, as from here it was possible to control trade right throughout the region. In that time goods, or even whole boats, were dragged between the two seas to save sailing the long and sometimes dangerous journey around the Peloponnese. In the late nineteenth century the Corinth Canal was built. We stopped nearby and walked on the bridge over the canal. At that point the earth walls of the canal are quite deep and steep, their starkness broken only by a lone eucalyptus tree.

In cities in many other parts of the world new buildings have been erected on top of the old ones. Fortunately in much of the Greek world the new cities have been built beside the former ones, leaving archaeologists the opportunity to excavate and display the ancient sites. Corinth is such a place.

The Temple of Apollo stands in the middle of Corinth and is the only major Greek building which remains. A theatre and forum are among the many Roman buildings which are accessible for inspection. Eléni pointed out the various styles of Greek columns, the Corinthian ones with their floral capitals having originated right here. She reminded us that St Paul lived here for one and a half years, working as a tent-maker and arousing the ire of some for persuading people to worship God in ways contrary to the law. She took us to the place where Gallio, the Roman official, would have stood to pass judgment on Paul and his accusers.

Sometimes during a tour a particular meal stands out in my memory. The lunch we had that day in a roadside restaurant called Haini Anesti was one of those. Set in a small but nicely treed valley, it is run by a helpful and happy family. In the customary way we sat under a large vine-covered pergola to eat barbecued lamb and fresh local vegetables with lots of good wine.

The archaeological sites we had seen so far on mainland Greece had been from the classical period, from about 500 BC through the Roman era—the times of Socrates and St Paul. We were next to visit a hillside site at Mycenae, not far south of Corinth, from the period of ancient Greece—the time of Ulysses and before. It flourished for a thousand years or more up to 1200 BC. King Agamemnon, a Greek leader in the Trojan War, was one of its last rulers. In the *Iliad* he is described by Homer, who also depicted Mycenae as well built and rich in gold. We entered the city through the admirable Lion Gate—two lions are carved into the lintel. As we stood on the hilltop looking down the picturesque valley towards the sea, Alison commented, 'Can't you imagine Clytemnestra sitting right here, watching Agamemnon returning in triumph from Troy and saying, "I'll kill him the moment he walks in the door"?' Some of us needed her to explain that Clytemnestra, unlike Ulysses' faithful wife Penelope, had taken a lover while Agamemnon was away.

Southeast of Mycenae we came to Epidaurus, and like all good tourists we were most impressed by its huge Greek theatre. It dates from the fourth century BC, is the best preserved in the country and can seat many thousands. Noted for its marvellous acoustics, someone has kindly marked the spot at the front where a speaker or singer can best be heard. At the group's insistence Gough walked to that spot and, with us seated around the auditorium, gave his 'Men and women of Australia' call.

When Barry Jones visited Epidaurus the following year, he had Margaret from Ballarat in the group. Margaret is a mezzo-soprano who once belonged to an opera company in England and has sung opera in Australia. She walked confidently to 'the spot' and burst into a rendition of 'O Mio Babbino Caro' from Puccini's opera *Gianni Schicchi*. There were several other groups in the theatre at the time, including people from Italy and France. After listening intently, the Italians applauded the loudest and everyone called for an encore. She obliged with 'Plasir d'amour', and this time the French led the applause.

Epidaurus was also regarded as the birthplace of Asclepius, the god of healing, and this place was a great healing centre. The museum has a fascinating collection of instruments and equipment used by physicians and surgeons all those centuries ago. Dr Hugh was one of the medical people in our group who examined these in detail.

Travelling in the Peloponnese is wearying. Some sites require quite a bit of climbing and the warm Mediterranean sun takes its toll. We were glad each evening to find refuge in the practical hotels appropriately located for travellers' needs. They tend to be concrete and tile but comfortable, with lots of sitting areas and surrounded by gardens which give a pleasant feel. I don't care very much for the buffet meals they serve, but I guess that makes catering easier and people do have a choice. Certainly I looked forward to putting my feet up each evening and washing the dust away with a refreshing drink. Our travellers could be seen gathering in small groups on balconies and lawns, many of us having taken enthusiastically to the aniseed flavoured ouzo so favoured by the Greeks.

The places we had visited so far on the Peloponnese were on the eastern coast. Olympia is on the western side, so it takes a rather rugged journey over the mountainous peninsula to get there. Fortunately the modern town of Olympia does not encroach on the ancient site. We were able to walk around it in quietness and feel something of its historic splendour.

Olympia was famous for its Temple of Zeus and more particularly for the golden statue of Zeus by Phidias which it contained. The statue was one of the Seven Wonders of the

Ancient World. We found that there was little of the temple still standing and the statue had disappeared centuries ago, but there is much else that is left and we were able to identify many of the other buildings, including those for the Olympic Games. With Sydney about to host the modern Olympics there was heightened interest for our group in seeing the original site.

The main Olympic stadium is almost intact. As we entered through the main archway the running track was obvious before us. I must admit that quite a bit of effort has gone into maintenance of the banks and the track, and it does appear as if races could be held there again at any time. Some of our men stood along the starting line, someone called 'go!' and they were off. They didn't run too badly for a batch of old buffers, but I had to disqualify them all. They had clothes on and that was not permitted in the real Games at Olympia.

Olympia itself is quite flat, although it is surrounded by hills. Trees have been allowed to grow among the ruins and it really is one of the most pleasant archaeological domains to visit. The canteens, the baths and living areas where the Games were held every four years for a millennium can all be viewed at leisure. It was very pertinent for us to see where the flame would be lit before making its way to Sydney.

We called at Patras on the northwest of the Peloponnese before taking the ferry back to the mainland. Tradition has it that the Apostle Andrew was crucified in Patras. The poor chap's remains are supposed to have been taken to Constantinople, then to Amalfi and later to Rome, only being returned to Greece fairly recently. In the process of transportation a bone was said to have arrived in Scotland. Anyhow, it was a good reason to build a handsome cathedral in Patras to house the

JUST ONE STAGE OF THE CLIMB TO THE TOP AT DELPHI. THIS IS THE TEMPLE OF ATHENA, AS GOOD A PLACE AS ANY TO THINK GOOD THOUGHTS.

remains of his X-shaped cross, and to give the name Andrew to every third boy born in the city.

It's convenient to leave the Peloponnese at this point and head for Delphi on the northern shore of the Gulf of Corinth. If Olympia is pleasant to visit, Delphi is hard, particularly for people like me who don't climb mountains very easily. But the place is magnificently built on the side of a very steep hill and can be seen in stages—it is my favourite site in Greece. Pilgrims used to come from all over the Greek world to consult the Oracle at Delphi. They would arrive at the shore and climb first to the Temple of Athena, where they would make offerings, purify themselves at the Castalian Spring, and then climb to the Temple of Apollo. Here a priestess, who had to be over the age of fifty, sat at the mouth of a cave and muttered prophetic words. These would be conveyed by a priest to the supplicant, who had paid well for the usually ambiguous advice. Charles had been here before and was particularly interested in the universal appeal of the Delphic Oracle. He pointed out, to some who were unsure, that the term 'oracle' here referred to the cave, to the priestess and to the prophecy itself. 'It seemed to work for the ancient Greeks' Charles noted. Certainly it dragged in the tourists—a skill which modern Greeks retain.

Eléni had us visit Delphi in the late afternoon when it was cooler and most tourists had already departed for Athens. Our overnight stay in Delphi was in a hotel where every room had the same magnificent view down to the sea that was enjoyed from the ancient city. An early morning visit to the Temple of Athena rounded out our Peloponnese journey.

Soon after we returned to Athens we joined the good ship *Arcadia* at the nearby seaport of Piraeus for a few days cruising the Greek islands. We all had cabins on the outside of the ship. Barely had we settled in before it was time for boat drill. We had problems fitting pieces of the life jackets together—all quite hilarious, really. The *Arcadia* belongs to a Greek line and spends its time cruising the Aegean Sea. It was not large compared to others, but it was comfortably understandable—getting to know it didn't take forever.

Nearly all those on board were from Western Europe. The captain and first officer were Greek while the program director was a full of life Venezuelan woman named Olga. Theodore, our cabin steward, was most attentive, as were the stewards in the dining room. When I saw the extensive buffet lunch laid out on that first day—every kind of seafood, meats and salads and a truly huge array of desserts—I realised that it would be easy to add a few kilograms on this voyage.

Early in the afternoon we came to the island of Mykonos, where we had to use tenders to go ashore. As part of the Cyclades group of islands, which lie in a circle around Delos, Mykonos was bound into the rich history and legend of ancient Greece. Centuries of attack and devastation have left the island with few historic monuments. The simple lives of the fishermen and their families have largely been taken over by tourism. The line of white-towered windmills, thatched roofs and flapping sails on a lee side ridge must be one of the Greek island images captured by thousands of cameras.

The narrow winding streets of Mykonos, constructed to shelter from strong winds, are quite alluring, with white houses, churches and shops with pretty products. I succumbed and bought a dear little lapis and silver pin in the shape of a pelican, plus the most beautiful necklace, silver with a lovers' knot and a single pearl. Pelicans are common on Mykonos, and one named Petros had been the island's mascot for twenty-nine years. He now resides, stuffed, in the excellent little museum. I also managed to pick up a pair of comfortable sandals which were to be great for the more relaxing days. Along the water's edge are the many rows of tables and chairs belonging to the bars. Most of our group seemed to home in on these and sat drinking ouzo and watching the brilliant colours of the setting sun. Then it was back on board for our first night at sea. I said goodnight to the team straight after dinner as I wanted to get the most out of our daily excursions. Some batted on till a late hour with the ship's entertainment.

The program on day two included a visit to Pátmos. Perhaps as an island it doesn't have the charm of Mykonos, but its attraction for many is the Holy Cave of the Apocalypse.

'I, John . . . was in the isle that is called Patmos . . . in the Spirit on the Lord's day and heard behind me a great voice' are the first words of the book of Revelation in the New Testament. Predictably the place where the voice was heard has been determined by tradition and a suitable church constructed around it. However, it does have a special aura and everyone seemed very satisfied by the visit. The day was fine, warm and sunny. Once again I noted in my diary: 'Sometimes I think we're in another world.'

Our second night on board was designated a 'Greek night'. Everyone was asked to dress in blue and white clothes—the colours of Greece. We all managed to oblige with varying degrees of success and hilarity—I wore a bright blue scarf over a white shirt. One of our men had a vividly striped shirt: 'It didn't look half as good on the hanger,' he claimed. We had a super Greek meal which was followed, appropriately, by a Greek concert.

The cruise gave us almost a full day on Rhodes. We commenced with a trip out to Lindos where the Acropolis of Lindos and the old crusader fort share a wonderful rocky cape. It seems that all the cruise ships arrive on the island on the same morning and immediately despatch their passengers here. Our coach became gridlocked in a veritable sea of others, with a totally inadequate system for parking or movement.

Rhodes has an ancient history—in fact it was the largest and most prosperous city–state of classical Greece. The most memorable feature of this era was a colossal statue to the god Helios, constructed after an attempted invasion by the Macedonians was repelled. It was thirty-two metres high, standing in the harbour of Rhodes and listed as one of the Seven Wonders of the Ancient World. It fell down about 200 BC and disappeared without trace, except that it reappears on the local postcards and souvenirs!

The recent history of Rhodes is far more apparent. The Knights of St John, made up of crusaders from many countries, had their headquarters here from the thirteenth century. They built some grand fortified buildings during the period up to the sixteenth century, when the threat of Turkish invasion persuaded them to move to Malta. After World War I Rhodes became part of Italy. By the time it was returned to Greek control after World War II there were well-constructed administrative buildings based on the knights' forts. Before leaving, the Italians erected a large plaque noting that they had exercised good and responsible government for those decades. The Greeks erected a similar sized plaque noting the role of the Italians but also that the island was rightfully part of Greece. Gough helped our participants by reading the first plaque, written in Italian, and the second, written in Greek. I guess that's one of the benefits of a classical education.

It was a formal dinner on the *Arcadia* that night. We gathered in the lounge for cocktails and an appropriate speech from the captain. Being a smaller ship and not entirely full as we were not quite in the high season, all the passengers were able to be seated in the dining room at the one time. It was a night of good fun, dinner culminating with a fully lit Bombe Alaska brought into the darkened room to the music from *Zorba the Greek*.

Our last full day of cruising included visits to Crete in the morning and to Santorini in the afternoon—how cavalier to spend so little time there! Both places justify a much longer stay to see the ancient ruins and to enjoy the pleasures of these Mediterranean islands. Nonetheless our time in Crete was spent almost entirely at the excavated palace of the Minoan civilisation at Knossos. For those of us who are astounded by things of great age this is quite an awe-inspiring place. While I love the whole archaeological site my favourite section is a mural of bright blue dolphins pictured with graceful arched bodies. Alison mused that it would have been nice to live in the wealth and beauty of the palace, but she didn't fancy having a sinister Minotaur roaming below.

Santorini, which is blindingly beautiful, is a volcanic ring with sheer cliffs rising 300 metres from the sea. There was time for us to see the recently uncovered civilisation at Akrotiri. Unlike earlier excavations which were done hurriedly and sometimes without a lot of finesse, the work is being done very carefully and under ideal conditions. Longer term this will be the most fascinating archaeological site of ancient Greece. The civilisation appears to have come to an abrupt end about 1500 BC with the eruption of the volcano from which the island is formed. We had a short time in the touristic but beautiful township of Thira, where we were able to take a much needed drink in one of the open bars at the top of the cliffs—we had the feeling that we were on the top of the world. I noticed Charles among those examining necklaces in the many jewellery shops that dotted the narrow streets—an eye for beauty as well as history! We hurried back to the cable car for a ride in the last car to get to the *Arcadia* on time. The next night we were to be in Turkey.

The Turkish seaport of Kusadasi is directly across from Athens on the Asian side of the Aegean Sea. Cruise ships call there and it is also a popular holiday resort area. It is a convenient place to arrive because it is near the old Greek cities of Ephesus, Smyrna and Pergamon. Immigration and customs were anything but convenient. We were able to continue our journey only after a complicated exchange of monies for port taxes, visas, porterage and what we might euphemistically call facilitation charges!

A visit to Ephesus, now known as Efes, leaves a sense of wonderment, but also some disappointment. This was the location of another of the Seven Wonders of the Ancient World, the Temple of Artemis, or the Temple of Diana as it was called later by the Romans. At one time the main feature of the city, it was eventually destroyed by the Goths. Goats graze around the few pieces of column remaining on waste land. Most guides avoid taking people to the site of the great temple, it looks so sad.

On the other hand the centre of the old administrative and commercial city is remarkably well preserved and has been carefully excavated and presented by archaeologists. The library is a great building, now skilfully restored to its original high structure with statues and friezes all in place. Houses and shops, including those of the famous silversmiths, can be inspected. It is easy to imagine the city's former grandeur. For some reason a lot of visitors seem to remember well the multi-holed latrine where the men sat for rather smelly meetings to discuss the affairs of the day.

Ephesus was an important city in ancient times, with some scholars believing that Homer could have lived there when he wrote the *Iliad*. It was a great city in the classical period of Greece when it was home to philosophers such as Heraclitus, who were contemporaries of Socrates. It became a great Roman

city—the main Roman city in Asia—and during that time
St John lived there and St Paul visited it. Another of the great
monuments of the city is the amphitheatre, which is larger than
the one at Epidaurus, although it does not have the same
acoustic qualities. I understand that Margaret from Ballarat
gave a good rendition of Handel's *Largo,* and Barry Jones
provided a dramatic reading of the story from the New Testament describing how the silversmiths, who made shrines for the
Temple of Diana, came screaming into this theatre protesting
against the preaching of St Paul.

While Gothic invaders pillaged Ephesus in the third
century, it soon became an important Christian centre. A great
church, dedicated to St John, was built on the hill overlooking
the site of the Temple of Diana. This is another important site
which most visitors miss. All tourists, however, are herded into
the pretty little site on the other side of the city which a German
nun claimed was revealed to her as the home of the Virgin Mary.
'Perhaps,' we would say, but the Turkish sales force takes full
advantage of it.

We stayed on the top floor of the Hilton Hotel in Izmir. This
is the modern Turkish city on the site of the ancient Greek city
of Smyrna. Most of the buildings are modern and it seems to
be a progressive city. From our window we could see the fort
built by the army of Alexander the Great, which is now in a
park-like setting on top of the highest hill.

I was looking forward to visiting Pergamon—or Bergama,
as it's now called—particularly as we had seen the Altar of Zeus
displayed so magnificently in the Pergamon museum in Berlin.
The altar was sometimes listed among the Seven Wonders of
the World. The site of the ancient city has its own splendour,

though on the day we were there the weather was bad—very wet and slippery. Pergamon is an acropolis and totally different to Ephesus, or any of the other old Greek cities we have seen. The place where the Altar to Zeus stood in its temple is now just a flattened platform, but I discovered that it had a great view over the valley. We noted that Pergamon had one of the seven churches addressed by St John in the Apocalypse. He referred to the Altar of Zeus as 'Satan's seat'—well, I guess not everyone would be pleased with it.

The route taken by the Barry Jones' group the year following us was a little different. We both came by Gallipoli, but the story will be easier to follow if I take you the way he went.

We had been travelling north from Kusadasi, where we landed in Turkey. From Pergamon it is a further twenty kilometres to the ancient city of Troy, which is perhaps best known to us from Homer's legend of the Greeks invading the city by means of a wooden horse. Agamemnon, from Mycenae, was the leader of the invading forces and Ulysses was there, about to take his legendary journey before going back to the faithful Penelope. There is probably some factual basis to the story, the siege and battle taking place about 1300 BC.

Archaeologists started excavating Troy more than a hundred years ago. Nine levels of occupation dating between 4000 BC and 1300 AD have now been identified. It is a wonderful place for those seriously interested in archaeology but compared to sites like Ephesus, there is very little to see. Our group sat around in a small arena while Barry read about the battle from a new translation of the *Iliad*. A group of Turkish school children joined the audience for the presentation, which became very animated. They probably couldn't understand a word he was saying, but they were most intrigued. A big wooden horse has now been built to attract tourists, who otherwise may find the ruins not so impressive—and only rarely does an Australian politician perform.

Standing on the site of ancient Troy it is possible to look a few miles across the water and see the monuments at Gallipoli. The water between the two is the Dardanelles, the strait leading from the Aegean Sea to the Sea of Marmara. This in turn leads to the Bosphorus, which is another strait leading to the Black Sea. In the days of the ancient Greeks the Dardanelles was known as the Hellespont and was significant in history and legend. The legendary hero Leander swam it each evening to meet his lover. Lord Byron had swum the four miles across the Hellespont to emulate Leander. Before diving in, Dr Hugh tried to identify where Byron would have commenced his swim. Mary and some of the others joined him, but alas they didn't match Byron in strength or enthusiasm.

Gallipoli is a place of pilgrimage for Australians. We recognise the battle fought there in 1915 as a symbol of our nationalism. There are always questions about the wisdom of the British having waged war in the Dardanelles, and dragging Australia and New Zealand into the fight. Each of our groups has come to Gallipoli with reverence. The memorial at Anzac Cove tells of the landing on 25 April. The scenes of that landing, with the ominous cliffs behind the beach, are well known. We were greatly moved by the words of Ataturk, inscribed now at Anzac Cove: 'Those heroes that shed their blood and lost their lives are now lying in the soil of a friendly country. You, the mothers who sent your sons from far away countries, wipe away your tears; your sons are now living in our bosom and are at

LONE PINE, GALLIPOLI. NO WAY WILL WE FORGET.

peace. After losing their lives on this land they have become our sons as well.'

The Australian memorial is at Lone Pine, on top of the cliffs. Many Australian and New Zealand graves are there and the names of hundreds of others are engraved on the monolith of the main memorial. The group stopped for a brief ceremony and wreath laying. Sir John Overall, an Australian army colonel who had served in the Middle East in World War II, military cross and bar, laid the wreath and relived the sadness as he recited the 'Ode to the Fallen'.

With the establishment of the modern republic in 1923, Ankara was chosen as Turkey's capital. It is 350 kilometres east of Istanbul and readily accessible by plane. It has a long history going back to the ancient Hittites and was later occupied by the Gauls, who established the city as the capital of Galatia. We took the opportunity of hearing about the modern and probably more volatile history of modern Turkey, having arranged for a speaker to tell us about the social and political scene in the country and its relationships with the outside world.

We continued further west by coach to Central Anatolia and Cappadocia, a wondrous place noted for its extravagant fairy-tale landscape. It is a landscape which made it possible for homes and churches—even whole villages—to be carved out of the rock. It was an area where very early Christianity had thrived. As we travelled through the ghostly terrain, Gough's sister Freda talked to our group about the early church in these parts. For the following year's tour Barry read descriptive parts from St Paul's epistle to the Galatians. Both added life and relevance to a dry countryside.

Our days in Cappadocia were full of discovery. The houses carved into the soft rock of the hillsides, and particularly the churches, are just fascinating to visit. Some are big enough to hold large numbers of people. There are many spectacular valleys with hundreds of phallic-like natural towers.

While the fairyland hills and towers make the greatest visual impact, equally interesting are nearby underground towns. These were constructed below a quite level countryside. Naturally formed caves were enlarged to provide catacomb style accommodation for hundreds of people, together with churches and other community facilities. They were built in the early centuries AD, largely with their defence capacity in mind. I had to content myself with a glimpse into one of these underground towns, while the more agile ventured down several levels. Father Jim discovered that he wasn't quite agile enough to have lived in that era. He got stuck in one of the tunnels, and it was only with some pushing and pulling that he was able to get out.

CAPPADOCIA SHOWS THAT FAIRIES DON'T
NEED A GARDEN.

In the evening we went to a great carved cavern to see whirling dervishes performing their religious craft. In a circle were eight men dressed in long white skirts, white stockings and black shoes. The grand master stood in the centre and a music group to one side. Pivoting on one foot and pushing with the other, each commenced to spin, their skirts opening tent-like. All continually whirled to the music for about twenty minutes or so. It was quite hypnotic for the dervishes, and for us. One of the younger members was obviously not feeling well and the grand master gently removed him from the circle. We stayed after the performance for a short time to hear the dervishes talk about the religious and spiritual significance of the experience. I don't think any of us planned to take it up!

Our journey finished in Istanbul, one of the most exciting cities in the world. As on many of our other tours we had arranged to spend several days at our last stopping place. First called Byzantium, then Constantinople, it was the capital of the Byzantine Empire for a thousand years. Occupied by the Ottomans in 1453, it was the capital of the Ottoman Empire for the next 470 years. We visited the ostentatious palace of the sultans, with its harem and grand treasury buildings. It was a seemingly endless walk through silk-draped rooms. In the centre of the city magnificent St Sophia stands beside the Blue Mosque. Originally built as a Christian church, St Sophia was converted to a mosque after the Ottomans occupied the city, but now functions only as a museum. The more active of us— including Gough, who has always been so impressed by St Sophia—climbed to a top balcony where the whole interior of the former church can be seen. John, who was with him, commented that it was among the greatest buildings of Europe. Gough paused a moment, shook his head and said, 'No—*the* greatest.'

No short visit to Istanbul is ever enough. We visited the Grand Bazaar, the Spice Market and the amazing cisterns built by Justinian—there is just so much to see. We took a cruise along the Bosphorus, with an excellent commentary from our guide, and had dinner in a fish restaurant looking out onto the Black Sea. We went to a very good performance of the ballet *Sleeping Beauty* at the Ataturk theatre. Most things are named for Ataturk, the father of modern Turkey, and his image is ubiquitous. He stands out among world leaders of the twentieth century as a man who built a nation and worked hard to bring his country into the western world.

Part of Istanbul is in Europe, the other part in Asia. Traditions of both continents meld in its unique culture. To experience more of the eastern tradition we went to see belly dancing at the Karavanserai nightclub. There were skilled performers, men and women, dancing, singing and doing acrobatics. Some of our group indicated that they were not impressed—perhaps they thought the women were not properly clad. Four very voluptuous dancers were giving a very sensual performance when they announced that they wanted four men from the audience to join them. The prettiest one pounced on Father Jim. The next moment, to the horror of some, our priest was on stage, displaying a less pious disposition than usual as, with a great grin, he danced with the best of them.

I can't leave our travels in Greece and Turkey in the dubious environment of an Istanbul nightclub, though it was lots of fun. Instead I should take you back to the three people who have provided continuity for our travels in these parts—Ulysses, Socrates and St Paul—and give them the last words.

Socrates was inspired by a special quest: 'To spend my life searching for wisdom, and in examining myself and others,' was how he explained his ambition to the people in Athens.

St Paul had a greater ambition, though he was influenced by the ideas of Socrates. 'Though I have all knowledge and all faith so that I could move mountains, and have not love, I am nothing,' he wrote to the people of Corinth.

For those of us of advancing years I find real inspiration in the words of Ulysses. He had returned to Penelope, after Troy and his epic journey, and ruled his country well. One day he gathered together his old sailor mates and urged them to set off with him once again, this time to sail across the Mediterranean and see what was out in the Atlantic Ocean. Ulysses' thoughts are expressed brilliantly in our language by Tennyson.

How dull it is to pause, to make an end
To rust unburnished, not to shine in use!
I cannot rest from travel . . . come my friends
Tis not too late to seek a newer world
To sail beyond the sunset and the baths
Of all the western stars . . .

There is something wonderful about the classics—and something worthwhile in a classical education.

LANDS OF THE DRAGONS

DRAGONS ARE FOUND AS mythical creatures throughout many parts of Asia. The five-toed Chinese dragon appears in many stories and the dragon is one of the twelve creatures, each reigning for twelve months, in the Chinese zodiac. In Thailand and other countries of South East Asia, the dragon appears in legend and art, and unexplained events are attributed to it. The Asian dragons are not the ferocious fire-eating monsters of the west. Instead they guard temples, entertain at festivals and provide wonderful images for silk designs and art and crafts of all kinds.

During the 1990s we organised tours that visited nine different Asian countries. Our most frequent destination was Thailand, followed by Indonesia. We had two tours into Bhutan, where the national symbol is the dragon, and our groups flew in with Druk (meaning dragon) airlines. We had four tours in China and I want first to tell you about one of those which Gough and I led.

China has a special interest for my husband. His first visit was in 1971 at the invitation of the People's Institute of

IN THE ARMS OF THE DRAGON.

Foreign Affairs to discuss issues relating to China and Australia. I was fortunate to be with him on a number of later visits when he helped develop relations between the two countries. However, our three-week ISP tour gave both of us the opportunity of appreciating China in a different way and to visit several different places.

Because of all those earlier contacts, our relationship with China's officials was good. The Consul General in Sydney invited the whole group to his home the evening before we flew out for China. It was a generous gesture and a good opportunity for all to meet in comfortable circumstances. We experienced some traditional Chinese hospitality.

The next morning our excited group gathered at Sydney airport. John was the manager of the tour, assisted by Helen

Wong, an expert in China travel. Though still a British colony at that time, Hong Kong was to be an interesting start for the journey.

The hotel in Hong Kong proved to be indicative of the accommodation we experienced over the next three weeks—modern, good-sized rooms, facilities which always worked, and good meals with both Chinese and international cuisine. The hotel provided us with an excellent conference room for our first morning, when we were able to have personal introductions and Gough gave the group a broad history of China as an ancient and modern land. The morning finished with Garth Hunt, our Australian Consul, talking about the 150 years of British and Chinese history in Hong Kong and the program for the return to Chinese ownership. He pointed out that Hong Kong had six million people in an area half the size of the ACT. It has no natural resources, just labour and the less definable resource of 'drive'.

The afternoon saw us on a city tour which took us, via cable car, to The Peak. At Stanley markets I bought a copy of a Chanel bag and a silk shirt at good prices, and picked up bottles of juice and water for later—so necessary in such a steamy climate. The afternoon ended with a sampan ride in Aberdeen harbour, which was ringed with modern luxury yachts.

We discovered that the Chinese refer to westerners as 'big noses' and we enjoyed addressing each other by that title. An expression which we learned early was *ma ma hoo hoo*. It is used widely across China in a range of situations, and means something like 'so so'. We were rather impressed by the harmony of the expression and it became widely used within the group.

Two vivacious travellers, Jan and Jill, came up with the 'Ma Ma Hoo Hoo Song', which was added to in each new city. As I read it again I realise that it was not entirely good poetry, but it was certainly good fun. Sung to the tune of a popular song of fifty years ago that started with the words 'Down by the station early in the morning, see the little engines standing in a row', Jan and Jill's song began:

Down at the airport early in the morning
See the little aeroplanes standing in a row,
All the big nose tourists setting off for China
Ma ma hoo hoo, off we go.

First stop is Hong Kong, sailing in a sampan
See the people shopping, spending high and low,
Buying on the mountain, then in Stanley market
Ma ma hoo hoo, off we go.

While I can speak well of most hotels and services in China, airports and air transfers often left something to be desired. I learned to keep my fingers crossed when a plane journey was indicated and to prepare for hours of sitting and waiting. The flight to Hangzhou was such a journey, but the reception we received on arrival at the hotel made up for the travel diffi-culties of the early morning.

Hangzhou is noted for the beauty of the city and the surrounding hills. Outside our hotel was a lovely red granite fountain and engraved in large letters on it was 'Southern hills appear in sight of a leisurely mind'. I pondered over it for a while. It seemed to be one of those oriental sayings which sound wonderful, but then you have to ask yourself 'what does that mean?'. Perhaps they lose something in the translation.

We visited the West Lake, a huge park much frequented by the locals, and one of the top ten scenic spots of China. We began to understand the benefits of a leisurely mind when we passed by a pavilion called 'Autumn moon over the calm lake'. We took a trip on a boat alighting at 'Crossing the rainbow', and later we went to the 'Pagoda of the Six Harmonies'. Visits to a tea plantation and a silk factory were also interesting, but less poetic.

Most of our travellers take a camera with them, and occasionally we have someone with a video. Ruth, a mathematician from Newcastle, had a video camera on this tour and I noticed that she was sometimes aiming it at strange objects. Some time after the tour we saw her final art work. One of her videos was dedicated to a study of Chinese garbage bins. I managed to travel through the country without taking much notice of these functional items, but she had captured a mixture of the most colourful and quaint creations, everything from a panda to a full moon.

Fortunately the journey to Wuxi was by coach, then by luxury ferry across another lake which, this time, we shared with numerous fishing boats. We had only a brief stop in this industrial city. After a late arrival, late dinner and shortened sleep, we were whisked away for visits to a freshwater pearl factory and one where they made clay figures—no free samples of either, unfortunately. The deputy mayor of Wuxi, a very confident young man who was keen to develop trading contacts with Australia, joined us for dinner and spoke to the group.

Naturally our Hangzhou and Wuxi experiences were added to our theme song:

Landing at Hangzhou, what a ghastly airport,
Stumble to the hotel feeling rather low,
Wow—there's a brass band, what a great reception!
Ma ma hoo hoo, off we go.

Passed through Wuxi, barely can remember,
Factories and smokestacks in the pouring rain,
Junks out on Lake Tai catching little whitebait
Ma ma hoo hoo, off we go.

I was looking forward to three nights in Shanghai, and our journey there was by train. This is the most populous city in the world's most populous country. It has the greatest concentration of industry and is the country's most important port. Its development took place in the nineteenth century when merchants and diplomats from western countries established themselves here, but their achievement has been dwarfed by the enormous growth which took place in the 1990s and continues.

In the days of western domination of Shanghai, European style buildings were constructed along the harbour front, separated from the water by an embankment known as The Bund. It is claimed that The Bund was fenced off and notices erected saying 'No dogs or Chinese permitted'. These days the Chinese are there in their thousands, particularly in the early mornings when there are many large groups doing tai chi and other gentle exercise or arts. There are also hundreds on the Bund practising western style ballroom dancing.

We stayed in the Peace Hotel, which is right on The Bund. It's a wonderful old-style hotel built in 1928 and somehow surviving intact through decades of enormous social and political change. The ultimate old world experience was on our first evening, when a jazz band played the fabulous music of my younger days. No one in the band was under sixty, and some were much older. Our party distinguished itself in the dancing after dinner. Alison and Robin showed that they were not only a knowledgeable couple, but very good dancers too.

In this city of enormous change we made a visit to one place that had had a key role in those changes—the House of the First Meeting of the Party. It was here in Shanghai that the first meeting of the Communist Party was held early in the century. It is now a small museum. It is said that Mao was at the meeting, but at that time did not play an important role. Who could have imagined the outcome, in only a few decades, of that meeting?

We went next to a children's palace, one of those excellent facilities the state provides for after-school and leisure-time activities. They are well staffed and the children learn useful skills in a safe and happy environment. The children put on a concert for us at which, to my great displeasure, Gough and John sat in the front row of seats and went to sleep. They did manage to stay awake that night at a superb performance of acrobatics.

An interesting visit of a different sort was to the newly developing Pudong, a huge industrial and commercial area. China is sufficiently authoritarian to plan and push ahead with a program of this size without the problems which would be faced in other countries. I could only hope that reasonable care would be taken of the environment and of the lives of the many families that were displaced. Walter Goode, our Consul-General in Shanghai, was able to give us more information about the history and development of the city—this was a study tour, remember! He spoke of the thousands who come in from adjacent rural areas each day hoping to get jobs on the construction sites. He told us of new housing programs which are planned on the basis of 2.5 square metres of space per person. 'What about sewerage?' someone asked him. 'Each family takes a daily visit to a central collection point with the chamber pot,' he explained. I was glad that our hotel, like many of the better offices and homes, had other arrangements.

The Chinese have a great predilection for ceremony, particularly for visiting dignitaries. Although Gough and I were travelling on diplomatic passports and our movements were known to the Australian and Chinese authorities, our visit was not an official one for the Australian government. Nonetheless, late one evening while we were still in Shanghai, John received word from a Chinese official of the plans for our arrival the following day in Beijing. Gough was to be met by their Foreign Affairs man and conveyed to the hotel, there would be a media conference and in the afternoon he would be received by the Vice President of China in the Great Hall of the People. It was a nice honour but fraught with diplomatic dangers. At breakfast the next morning, Gough and John got together with two of our other travellers—Sir Neil Curry, who had been Australian Ambassador in Japan, and John Richardson, who had been editor of the *Newcastle Herald* and chief of staff with the *Sydney Morning Herald*—to draw up an action plan. Sir Neil was to contact our ambassador and have him involved at every stage, John Richardson was to handle the media conference, and John Wellings, our tour manager, was to communicate with the Chinese officials. All worked out very smoothly. I am always grateful that we have had people travel with us who had the skills to help and advise in many and varied situations.

Our theme song continued to grow:

Touch down at Shanghai, thirteen million people,
All of them are dancing ballroom on The Bund,
Went to a jazz club, trumpeter was eighty
Ma ma hoo hoo, off we go.

Next stop is Beijing, capital of China
City squares and palaces lined up in a row,
Meeting us in Beijing is a pride of lions
Ma ma hoo hoo, off we go.

There were indeed lions to meet us at the hotel—mythical lions with people inside, and dragons too. We went to meet the Vice President at the Great Hall of the People. Suitably briefed by our ambassador, who also attended the meeting, Gough was able to support a number of issues that the Australian government had already raised with the Chinese. Kenneth and Berta from Tasmania had thoughtfully brought along a top quality blanket made from pure Australian wool, and they gave it to me to present to the Vice President. I hope that it keeps him warm on Beijing's cold winter nights, and that he has encouraged even a tiny proportion of China's 1.25 billion people to buy one.

Tiananmen Square—or the Gate of Heavenly Peace—is in the centre of Beijing. The Great Hall of the People and one of the entrances to the Forbidden City face onto the square. Beijing was the capital of China continuously from the time of

Kublai Khan (and Marco Polo) until the end of the Ming dynasty in 1912. It returned to being the capital under the People's Republic in 1949. The Forbidden City, where the extended families and courtiers of the emperors lived, is now a museum. It is no longer forbidden, but a brief introduction took us most of the morning.

John Richardson, who had helped with our media contacts, had a personal mission in Beijing. A relative from a previous generation had been an entrepreneur in China at the beginning of the twentieth century and had helped the imperial government in negotiations with England and the west, earning him the nickname of 'Chinese Morrison'. His most famous role had been to assist the Chinese delegation, albeit not too successfully, at the Versailles Conference at the end of World War I. John had the address of his relative's former home. From an old map he located the street, the name of which had since been changed. Several of our group went with him to explore. It was not possible to identify the exact house, but it was in a street formerly occupied by foreigners and a small Christian church still functioned there. John told me of the satisfaction he received from discovering something from a world he had heard about since childhood.

What did the rest of us think of Beijing? There was certainly a lot of well-planned development taking place—wide streets and grand buildings—and at that stage it was handling traffic well. It seemed to be a rather dusty or smoggy city, and it doesn't have the charm of the coastal cities like Shanghai and Hong Kong. The grandeur of Tiananmen Square and the buildings surrounding it was spoiled by our knowledge of those who were killed there in the demonstrations some years earlier.

The Ming tombs are not far out of Beijing and our visit there occupied another excellent morning. Some of the emperors' treasures are in a very interesting museum. We had lunch at the glossy Beijing Golf Club before journeying to the Great Wall of China. It is now more than 2000 years since construction of the wall was started in the vain endeavour to keep the Mongols out, and the part near Beijing has been restored to excellent condition. Most of our group walked on the wall, although a few of us chose to see this extraordinary sight from a nearby vantage point. With such an enormous population there will always be a large number visiting the country's number one tourist attraction.

Waiting and waiting at the Beijing airport,
Why we have to wait there no one seems to know,
Alison and Berta try to catch their own plane
Ma ma hoo hoo, off they go.

We had been fortunate over the years that, at least until this day, there had been very few difficulties with flights and transport generally. A few stuck coaches and minor delays, but nothing to compare with the fiasco of trying to leave Beijing to fly to the ancient imperial city of Xi'an. In a country which can manage enormous enterprises it is amazing that there could be such a foul-up in moving thirty people from one major city to another. We had left our hotel before lunch to go to the airport for a plane which was scheduled to leave at 12.25 pm. On arrival we started the inevitable waiting—12.25 came and went and still we waited. The amazing thing was that no one knew why or what was happening, or if they did they were not telling us. Helen Wong managed to get access to airline staff behind the front desk, but could get no help or comfort. Eventually, late in the evening, one piece of information emerged—there would be no more flights to Xi'an that day.

Our group spent the night in a hotel near the airport and returned next morning. Still no information about our flight. This really was a tour leader's nightmare. We phoned the Australian Embassy and one of the Mandarin speaking staff came out to help. Still no joy. It is interesting how a group reacts to a situation like this. Rumour, of course, is rife and there were some amazing stories circulating about the cause of our dilemma. Some people found games to play. I discovered one of the reasons Robin knows so much about things—he sat, hour after hour, reading a book of philosophy, though his wife Alison was not so composed. Sometime during the afternoon Alison had discovered that a flight for Xi'an was leaving from another gate. Alison and Berta decided that they had had enough of waiting round and would try and board this plane. Despite the fact that they hardly blended with the local population they nearly succeeded in getting a seat. Alas for them they were discovered and returned to our waiting group. It was, in fact, at 5.45 pm on day two that we eventually left Beijing for Xi'an. Whether the stuff-up was with the Chinese agency which had responsibility for making the reservation or whether the problem was with the airline, we will never know.

The delay meant that our time in Xi'an was limited—a pity as it is quite extraordinary. The ancient capital was started about 200 BC by the Ch'in dynasty—the dynasty from which the name 'China' comes. The city wall is still intact and it's from here that the old Silk Road commences between China, the Middle East and Europe. The main interest for most visitors, though, is to see the terracotta warriors. There are about 7000 of them lined up in marching formation. Remarkably lifelike, they were buried until 1974, but are now revealed and covered by a shed as large as a big aeroplane hangar. It is claimed that the warriors were to accompany the emperor into the afterlife, and so were buried along with him. Although we had all seen pictures of the entombed warriors, most were not prepared for the impact that the sight of them would have. Our group was ecstatic at the unique spectacle of this great entombed army.

In an attempt to redeem the time we had lost, the authorities provided a police car to get our bus through the traffic as quickly as possible. As our next stopping place was Guilin, where we were to have two nights simply to enjoy the beautiful countryside, I was looking forward to the group regaining its composure. And I was very relieved when our flight there took off on time and without incident.

Next stop at Guilin, land of lovely mountains
Hotel by the river where the waters flow,
Sailing through the gorges, climbing through the caverns
Ma ma hoo hoo, off we go.

The secret to the beauty of Guilin is that it is in a vast area of limestone. There are limestone caves in the hills around the town, and the countryside is fertile and green. But the best part is the columns sticking up like giant stalagmites out of the waters of the river. We had a lovely hotel on the water's edge with most of the rooms looking out over the river where the next day we were to cruise. This was the highlight—it was much

Merrily, merrily, merrily, life is just a dream in Guilin.

wider than I had expected and the sheer cliffs and columns just seem to go on and on. We had a visit to the Reed Flute Cave on the edge of town in the afternoon—nothing to compare with Jenolan, but I must say we have nothing in Australia to compare with the gorgeous water scenery of Guilin.

Lastly at Guangzhou, say goodbye to China
Tucking into dim sims, tummies fit to blow
Up the little gangplank, dripping perspiration
Ma ma hoo hoo, off we go.

Our last internal flight was down to Guangzhou, a city that we had always known as Canton. It is China's sixth largest city with a population of about six million, and is on a river delta behind Hong Kong. As a great trading city it shares something of the cosmopolitan flavour of Shanghai. The Cantonese are famous for food and they like it fresh, so it was not surprising to see a woman with a pair of large live frogs, restrained by strings around their waists, being taken home for dinner. Such sights did not put us off our food and in fact we really made the most of our farewell dinner, with lots of interesting dishes and good humour. It was a convenient place to end our journey through China, though it was the middle of the year and very hot and humid. It took only a little over two hours by hydrofoil to get back to Hong Kong, where our journey had commenced. China will undoubtedly loom large on the world's stage in the twenty-first century. I was glad we had been able to learn more about it at first hand.

I have already described Jan and Jill, the authors of our song, as a vivacious pair. I was delighted to meet them on this tour and have enjoyed occasions since when they have travelled with us. They met at university and have continued their friendship over many years, although Jill lives in Sydney and Jan on a few acres just beyond the Blue Mountains. It was their first trip to China although they knew much about it from their studies. They told me that the historic sites, including the terracotta warriors, were the most interesting parts of the itinerary for them.

Another of those in China taking her first tour with us was Clare from Melbourne. Clare had been a champion rower in her more youthful days and had rowed for Victoria in competitions. Now a widow, she preferred to travel in the comfort of a group. She was one of those people who always had a smile, appreciated everything and got on well with everyone. She had a wide knowledge of world affairs so was always good company at dinner or as we travelled. She later travelled to Thailand, Indonesia and Europe with ISP, and you will meet her again in South America.

Clare, like most of our other travellers, enjoyed shopping in the Asian markets. There is just such a great range of every imaginable item of clothing, jewellery and furnishings—you name it. And the prices are usually as attractive as the wares. On one of our Asian tours Clare appeared in a *very* smart slack suit. She was always well dressed but this was an outfit which attracted everyone's attention. It is always a case of buyer beware in these markets, though, for Clare tells me that she washed it when she got home and it became small enough to fit her six year old granddaughter.

While we were able to organise many tours into Thailand, Gough and I went only once as leaders. Because of a commitment in Australia we missed the first few days, but let me describe the whole tour so that you have a more complete picture.

One of the reasons for having frequent Thailand tours was the relationship that we had formed with another of those participants from the 1988 International Adult Education Conference in Australia. Professor Dr Ratana Poompaisal was in the Faculty of Education at Chulalongkorn University in Bangkok, Thailand's oldest and most prestigious university. In addition to advising on the best places to see, she has always arranged top lecturers to talk to our groups. Ratana is also a delightful person with a great sense of fun and relates so warmly to the participants.

Most flights into Bangkok from Australia arrive late in the evening, and that's helpful for us as Bangkok is a log-jam of traffic during the day. Our accommodation was at the guest house of Chulalongkorn University, a veritable oasis in the centre of such a crowded city. The Thai Association of University Women, of which Dr Ratana was the Vice President, organised a welcome ceremony and the program of lectures which would give us a background to this rapidly developing country with a population already of about sixty million.

Professors of history, sociology and medicine talked with our group on the first two mornings. Our historian explained that Thai writing developed only in the twelfth century, and that was at Sukhothai, in the country's north. Few documents remain in Thailand from the eras before the development of the Bangkok kingdom just over 200 years ago. The best records of Thai life and historical events were made by visiting Europeans and these records have been deposited in European libraries, so he had spent much of his career in Europe learning about Thailand.

There are a few things in Bangkok which every visitor must do. The most spectacular visit is to the old palace complex which includes the Temple of the Emerald Buddha. The Buddha is not emerald but jade and stands on a high golden pedestal. The King of Thailand comes each season and changes the clothes of the Bhudda, not an easy task given the height of the statue from the floor. The interior of the temple is laden with gold and precious stones, while the exterior bears a mixture of semi-precious stones and gold leaf. The Temple of the Emerald Bhudda must be among the most beautiful and remarkable buildings in the world.

Our afternoon visit was to the Population and Development Centre, which may sound boring but it wasn't. This non-government agency is headed by the charismatic Dr Meechai, and it tackles some of the most pressing problems, including overpopulation, faced by Thailand along with other developing countries. Dr Meechai met and talked with our group. He had been educated in Australia and his accent is warmly Australian. The establishment of child-care centres and nutrition programs has been high on the agenda for the foundation, but its major contribution has been in the area of adult education. For example, Meechai, through clever use of the media, has broken down taboos around contraception. The budget cafés where people can get help with nutrition and family planning are called 'Cabbages and Condoms'. He finds reasons for encouraging men to attend vasectomy clinics—those attending on 26 January are able to celebrate Kangaroo Day by having a quick operation. It was interesting to compare Thailand's wide encouragement of family planning with China's more authoritarian one-child policy.

The major part of our Thai tour was in the north, and we travelled by coach with a number of stops on the way, the first of these near the Bridge on the River Kwai. The remains of the old Burma Railway, which was built by forced Thai labour and Allied prisoners of war is here. It takes only about two hours from Bangkok to reach the bridge and the nearby Australian War Cemetery. If there is one thing that reminds us of the stark reality of a war which is still within the memory of so many living Australians, it is to visit a cemetery such as this. As we stopped there one of our group walked deliberately to a particular row and grave and stooped in front of it. Most of the group wandered through quietly, commenting on a name or an age. One woman remained on the coach—it was too much for her to face the sadness of finding the graves of three close friends of her youth.

The train runs for some thirty-two kilometres past the bridge on the River Kwai, and most of our groups have taken that journey. The track runs beside the river and crosses trestle bridges similar to the one depicted in the Academy Award winning film. The setting of the book and film is right here, though the details are fictitious—the bridge was actually destroyed by aircraft bombing. The book may be fictitious but the horror, pain and suffering were real. Just past the end of the railway is Hellfire Pass, which was built with enormous loss of Australian life. Our travellers have found it very moving to stand in that fatal and now isolated cutting. It has a memorial to Australian soldiers and is the resting place of Edward 'Weary' Dunlop's ashes. Strangely, the area near the bridge is quite beautiful. Our group stayed in a small resort called Prasopsuk, with little bungalows set in a beautiful garden. Meals were taken on low tables on a floating restaurant. It was a wonderful place to relax and reflect away from the bright lights of Bangkok.

The journey to Chiang Mai continued north with stops at Ayutthaya, Sukhothai and Lampang. Each had been the centre of a separate kingdom in older times, and the ruins of the ancient cities have been preserved in national parks. Visits in the early morning or late in the day have a special charm as the light reflects from the lakes and from buildings that were glorious centuries ago.

The main part of our program in northern Thailand was based in Chiang Mai. When King Mengrai established the city over seven hundred years ago he called it simply 'new city', which, in the Thai language, is Chiang Mai. It was a completely walled city and many parts of the wall remain, as does the moat around it. There were five gates through the wall and just outside one of them the king kept his white elephants—the gate was known, naturally, as the White Elephant Gate. It was right here, just outside the White Elephant Gate, that our home would be, the Northern Inn, for the next week.

Many Australians who visit Bangkok make the incorrect assumption that all of Thailand is like that. If only they were to spend time in one of the northern cities, like Chiang Mai, they would get a totally different impression of the country. It is easy-going, the people are friendly as well as beautiful, and there are so many interesting places to visit. Our travellers certainly enjoyed their time there, and you will see that they also learned a great deal.

Our program in the north of Thailand hinged around a very happy association developed over a number of years with Chiang Mai University. On our first morning Professor Annop introduced us to this region in the first of several lectures presented during the week by university staff. He explained how the north was the separate kingdom of Lanna until the middle of the nineteenth century. The area is proud of its different heritage, its architecture, nuances in the language and way of doing things. He spoke of the current issues of development and integration of the hill-tribe peoples, then of the tensions and opportunities in relation to Thailand's neighbours in Burma, Laos and China. I was impressed by his knowledge and openness. His colleague, Professor Prayad, was with him. We were to get to know them well.

Professor Prayad was responsible for food and nutrition education programs at the university. She has a great influence in the development of good nutrition through northern Thailand.

Later she gave us some useful pointers to understanding and cooking Thai food. The north is the land of sticky rice, the dishes are a little more spicy and they rarely use coconut milk. It seemed so easy when she threw the ingredients into the pan, gave them a quick stir and it all came out looking and tasting delicious. I have been fond of Thai food for many years but learned to appreciate it even more during our stay. I've cooked some of Prayad's recipes at home with some success.

Thailand is predominantly a Buddhist country and we learned a little more about their religion from Professor Sang, who had worn the saffron robes of a monk for eighteen years before taking a lecturing post at the university. He outlined some of the main principles of the faith, and told of spending a year studying in England. 'I went to a Christian church every Sunday, and understood a lot more about Buddhism,' he said with a soft smiling voice. He pointed out that for some, Buddhism is a transcendental experience, for others it is a moral and legalistic basis for society, and for many a sort of good luck system. I could see how he could perceive the same features in other religions.

A friend who had travelled Asia a great deal once told me that Chiang Mai's night bazaar was the best and most inter-esting market in Asia, and I was looking forward to checking it out. We travelled there in the standard public transport of northern Thailand, the *songtau*—Thai for 'two rows'. These are overgrown utilities, each with a canopy and two rows of seats in the back. Fortunately I was able to have a front seat beside the driver. The bazaar is a festival of glowing colours and bright lights, along with clothes of every description, arts and crafts, 'antiques', foods and novelties. And enormous happy crowds, many of them tourists but these are far outnumbered by the friendly locals.

Only a few yards around the corner from the bazaar is a different world. A traditional Thai-style house—up on stilts, oiled teak walls, polished floors, and topped with a steep pitched roof—in the quietness of a large and lovely garden. It houses the Whole Earth restaurant where we adjourned for a dinner of the local dishes. Our travel back to the hotel was by tuk-tuk. I'd seen them often in Bangkok but never thought I'd ride in one. They are a motor scooter with a covered seat at the back for two people, though you sometimes see six Thai people in one. It was breezy, noisy and a bit scary, fitting the character of Chiang Mai. Anne told me of one tour in which they lined up eight tuk-tuks to take a group back to the Northern Inn. When they were all ready John called 'go'. The drivers thought, or decided, that it was a race—it was a windswept and frightened group that was delivered to the hotel in record time.

One of the other pleasant things to do in Chiang Mai is to visit the many craft villages out of the main part of the city. Umbrellas are made using the traditional method of pulping wood to make paper and then painting it with sticky resin paints. Silver and brass workshops are nearby to woodcarvers and silk weavers. My favourite workshops were the Thai celadon kilns. I like those traditional green ceramics, and made a purchase of two sauce spoon rests. A large purchase!

I often remember a visit that we made to the Neanna Gallery. Patricia Cheeseman Neanna came from England but has spent her life studying and collecting Thai and Laotian fabrics, and lectures about them at the university. Her collection and workshop in suburban Chiang Mai was of great interest to us all, with her unique woven designs and patterns of universal appeal. I commissioned a silk jacket which is still a favourite for the opera.

We have a guide in Chiang Mai who has helped us with our travels many times, particularly when we wanted out-of-town visits. Malinee makes arrangements that flow very smoothly. Her constantly smiling face, typical of the beautiful young women of northern Thailand, always made us feel quite at ease. Malinee held a degree and postgraduate qualifications and was a director of her own company. When she was in her mid-twenties she went to Sydney to spend some time in the ISP office. When Anne took her to the bus station in Sydney to catch a bus to Brisbane, the ticket seller explained: 'If she is under fifteen she will need permission from her parents to travel.' Ah, the youthfulness of Thai women . . .

Malinee took us to Doi Suthep, the great mountain that watches over the city. It is a steep and somewhat hazardous drive but the views, and particularly the temple on top, are grand. A dragon lies on each side of the huge flight of stairs leading from the bus park to the temple. They are friendly, protective dragons, but we chose to go up in the funicular. The golden pagoda dominates the temple compound and there are pleasant pavilions where we could sit and take in the breezes, the views and a cool drink. It is a place that the Thai people like to visit, probably for the sense of serenity and security that we experienced there too.

We had visits into the valley of Mae Sai, beside Doi Suthep. Here the rich rainforest grows on the side of steep hills where the water feeds fast-flowing streams. Orchids grow to perfection and we called at one of the farms that cultivate them for market. It is an area where elephants were traditionally used for harvesting teak logs, but the timber industry is largely a thing of the past. We stopped to see the elephants bathing in the river and many of our group went for a short ride, although sometimes we have arranged for longer treks along the mountain tracks. There are several agreeable resorts in the valleys, places frequented more by Thai people than foreign tourists. Cabins are in exquisite mountain gardens and the restaurants serve great Thai food and cool drinks in a luxuriant setting. We met Kringthong, another delightful young Thai woman who over the years has helped us arrange group visits to the valley. I made a note that I would love to come back and stay for a few days in the company of people like Kringthong and simply relax in a wonderful world . . .

Dr Chot, the president designate of the university, as well as a dozen or more of the senior administrative and academic staff, had been to Australia during the previous couple of years, and we had arranged their study programs. We were somewhat surprised, however, when the university organised a banquet in our honour. It was attended not only by our group but a large number of the university's senior staff and the civic dignitaries of Chiang Mai. The location was the great hall of the university. At the end of the high-pitched roof were the crossed horns indicative of northern, or Lanna, Thailand. A profusion of orchids decorated the room to perfection. It was a memorable night, but also a useful one. The various speeches gave us some interesting insights into issues in education and development in Thailand. Gough responded with a coverage of the United Nations Treaties relevant to these same issues, many of which were still awaiting agreement by both Australia and Thailand.

Chiang Mai was readying itself for the main event of the year—the Loi Kratong Festival. This is a time celebrated all over Thailand, but its origins are in the north. A *kratong* is a floating wreath, made out of a cross-section of banana plant and decorated with flowers, an incense stick and a candle. 'Loi' means 'to float', so Loi Kratong means simply to float wreaths. The festivities are held at the time of the full moon in November, which marks the end of the monsoon season. Rural life is still dependent on the rain and, in a country where irrigation is practised, on the flow of the rivers. Loi Kratong is not strictly a Buddhist festival, but rather a spiritual acknowledgment of the importance of the rivers—thanks are given for the good flow from the rains just finished and atonement made for any misuse of the water. Well, that's the underlying significance but, as in other festivals in other countries, it is now a cause for a general celebration. I was really pleased we were at Chiang Mai for this special season.

While it is always a public holiday and celebrations go on for several days, the core of Loi Kratong is to take a *kratong* to the river on the night of the full moon and, with due ceremony, float it away. Our *kratong*s had been made by students at Chiang Mai University, so we knew that we had the real thing. Like thousands of Thai people and other visitors, we planned to have dinner by the river so that at the appropriate time we could all take our *kratong*s and float them. The manager of the hotel thought we should not go in ordinary clothes and supplied us all with the sort of simple cotton clothes that were traditionally worn at such festivals. I must say we looked rather good. Naturally, I have mine still. I'm a great hoarder of sentimental things.

Before we left for the river by *songtau*, Anne told us a few things we needed to be careful about. On a similar night a few years earlier, Dorothy, one of that tour group, had taken along a candle in a ceramic bowl, one about as big as a coconut. Dorothy had seen small candles like that burning in shops and on the street, and she thought a big one would be nice for the centre of the table. When everyone was seated the wick was ceremoniously lit—but alas, it was a fuse, not a wick. It was a giant firework that threw a fountain of sparks several metres into the air. Fortunately Annop was standing nearby as the first sparks took off. With quick reflexes he picked it up and threw it into the river. Even so, there were a few holes in the table-cloth and Annop's shirt.

Ours was a beautiful evening by the river. There were soft lights by which we ate our sticky rice and northern Thai curry. We were downstream from the centre of the city and the river became alive with candles lighting literally thousands of *kratong*s. Our group went to the edge to add ours to the collection, acknowledging our unity with the Thai people in their spiritual and practical lives. The smiling and supportive faces of Annop, Prayad and Malinee were above us. This is a land, a culture and a people to be loved. It's a land where even the dragons are friendly.

CHAPTER 8

INCAS, CONQUISTADORES

AND POLITICOS

GOUGH WAS THE FIRST Australian prime minister to visit Latin America when we called at Peru and Mexico in 1973, followed by an official visit to Brazil and Argentina a few years later. As Vice President of UNESCO's World Heritage Committee, Gough helped have nineteen natural and cultural sites in Argentina, Brazil, Peru and Bolivia inscribed on the World Heritage Register because of their outstanding universal value. We looked forward to leading an ISP group tour to South America, when we would attempt to provide an overall picture of that continent.

Planning a three-week tour to South America presented us with a problem because it is almost exactly twice the size of Australia with more than sixteen times our population. We chose places that would be representative of its histories, cultures and scenery. Argentina, Brazil, Peru and Bolivia would give us a range, and provide an insight into the enormous contrasts. Our itinerary would include two musts—Iguazú Falls and Machu Picchu.

In notes sent to the participants before we left we reminded them that Spain and Portugal sent *conquistadores* to establish colonies there in the sixteenth century. They found many civilised societies, of which the Incas were the most advanced, as well as nomadic tribes. *Libertadores* led movements for independence in the nineteenth century. The former Portuguese colonies formed the United States of Brazil, which is Portuguese speaking. It has about half the land mass of South America, and half of its population. The other half consists of nine independent Spanish speaking countries. The history of the continent since then has been influenced as much by *revolucionarios* as it has by *políticos*—an exotic blend of histories and cultures for us to explore.

We had asked our group to gather in the Piano Bar at Sydney airport after they had checked in. We had arranged for refreshments to be served and it would be our first meeting as a group. I was not the first to arrive in the Piano Bar for Charles, our Scottish born traveller, was already there—alone. Soon we were joined by Alison and Robin (who had already done the cryptic crossword), by Clare (who had flown up from Melbourne), by Dr Hugh and Elfie (I was glad that Hugh had some emergency medical gear with him), by Nell (who I was sure would have some dubious ditty on hand) and other familiar and happy faces of people who were ISP regulars. There were a few new travellers. Laurent and Jill, from Brisbane, were quiet and a little nervous. Nancy, a writer and a woman of style, was travelling alone. Anne and I were checking the numbers. There were to be thirty-two of us in the group, but we were one short. Just then Father Jim entered the room wearing a broad smile and a broad-brimmed Akubra.

Although Sydney and Buenos Aires, capital of Argentina, are at almost the same latitude, a direct air route between the two cities goes inside the Antarctic circle. The outward journey was mostly at night, but on our return we had wonderful views of the ice shelf and icebergs in a remarkably blue sea. Buenos Aires is probably the most European city of South America and there is much to make an Australian feel at home. But the differences are fascinating.

Certainly the Hotel Marriott, where we stayed, and the surrounding parks, elegant boulevards, plazas and public buildings had a familiar, comfortable feeling about them. Just down the road is the monument to those who fell during the war in the Malvinas, or Falkland Islands. It has an eternal flame and a permanent guard mounted—they look directly at the English Tower, which had been a gift from English residents in happier times.

People of English origin make up a significant minority in Buenos Aires. Marina Begg is from this group, and she made arrangements for us in Argentina, also helping us organise many aspects of the whole tour. She speaks perfect English without accent or affectation, although she is four generations from the land of her forebears. She constantly makes arrangements for other tour groups, but she regarded us as different and special. Certainly there were things that we wanted to do and see that were beyond the scope of most tourists. She worked largely in the background, but I was delighted to spend some time with her.

Marina had arranged for Diego to be our guide in and around Buenos Aires, and he took us first around the city square. Fronting the square are the main government buildings, and we were fascinated to see the balcony where Eva Perón made her famous and effective public appearances. We also saw where the liberator of Argentina and several other former colonies, José de San Martin, is buried in an annexe to the cathedral, not a chapel. He was not a Catholic and therefore was not allowed to be buried in consecrated ground. Perhaps the least forgettable thing in the square is where the mothers of the 'disappeared', those who were never heard of again after the last military dictatorship, come each week to walk. We visited La Boca, an Italian village of brightly painted corrugated iron buildings which houses an artists' colony. I bought a naive pen and ink drawing which rather charmingly includes the artist's dog and his small son.

Marina also arranged for Andrew Graham-Yooll, editor of the English language Buenos Aires *Herald*, to speak to our group. He is another fourth generation Argentinian of British descent, but a rather outspoken one. During the period of the military regime he fled the country after receiving death threats. He was able to give us an excellent survey of the social and political scene since the return to civil government—there are difficulties, but a good deal of optimism. In all four countries we were to visit on this tour, elected civil governments had replaced military governments within the previous decade. While we were in Buenos Aires, neighbouring Chile's General Pinochet announced his retirement and plans for his succession. I loved Andrew's headline in his paper summing up Pinochet's proposal for the future: 'Aprés moi, another moi'.

The next day we visited an *estancia* or cattle station in the *pampas,* owned and managed by a third generation Argentinian couple who were of totally French ancestry. We were able to see something of their highly productive agriculture and the traditional lifestyle. Diego was with us again, this time dressed

DIEGO NEVER CEASED TO INSTRUCT AND IMPRESS ME.

in the style of the *gauchos*, or cowboys, complete with a fine blue wool poncho, silver studded belt and blue beret. He really is an informative and charming guide. Marina had also arranged for us to visit a community school in the town near the *estancia*. It had primary and secondary departments, and one of its aims was to produce young men and women who, in addition to having a good general education, were computer literate and bilingual. All morning lessons are presented in Spanish, while all those in the afternoon, regardless of the subject, are presented in English. I have visited schools in many countries but I found this to be one of the most impressive.

The European nature of Buenos Aires was further shown during a visit to the ballet at the Teatro Colón—the Columbus theatre. John Cranko's *Onegin* was performed by top dancers, including Alessandra Ferri no less, in this theatre built in the grandest European style. On another evening we went to watch a uniquely Argentine tango show at the Casa Blanca, where each act provided high excitement.

A ninety-minute flight from Buenos Aires took us directly into Iguazú National Park. The border of Argentina and Brazil passes through the middle of the great Iguazú Falls. The reason you sometimes see different spellings and hear different pronunciations for the falls is the difference in the Spanish and Portuguese languages. We stayed for two nights at the lovely and traditional Hotel das Cataratas on the Brazilian side, but we viewed the falls from many angles in both countries. We ate in the modern Hotel Internacional on the Argentine side. Both hotels have superb positions looking at the falls from different perspectives.

Iguazú Falls are eighty metres high and nearly three kilometres long. By most standards they are the biggest in the world. Certainly they can be viewed and experienced from so many more vantage points than either Niagara or Victoria Falls. We looked at their many faces, we looked down from above, in places we went behind the water—a natural masterpiece to be enjoyed. During one of our encounters with the falls a young man, who was obviously blind, arrived with a young woman— his lover. They moved to a platform near the powerful force of the falls where the roar drowned all other sound. The spray covered their faces and hair, and I watched their joy as they experienced Iguazú together.

The walking and the viewing of the falls went on. Each bend produced another vision. At the bottom we suddenly came to a rainbow in front of the Devil's Throat, one of the most powerful parts of the falls. We had a dramatic boat ride in the river above the falls, then viewed them from a walkway where we could look down the Devil's Throat—all unbelievable. Around the world I have seen waterfalls, oceans spraying over rocks and mighty rivers, all showing the delights of wild water in nature, but to me Iguazú is nature's greatest celebration of water.

Most of us knew something of Iguazú from the 1986 film *The Mission,* set in the eighteenth century and staring Jeremy Irons and Robert De Niro. Although compressed in time and space, the story of the film is based on fact. It tells of the establishment of a Jesuit mission near the falls, and the conflicts with the Spanish and Portuguese authorities. There were in fact many missions in the area and a number of their ruins are now listed as World Heritage sites. The Jesuits were made to leave South America at that time, and were also banned from many countries in Europe.

The Jesuits eventually returned to South America, and we arranged for Dr Miguel Petty SJ to stay at Iguazú with us and tell us something of that era. As a modern time Jesuit he is a lecturer in history and sociology at a university in Argentina, and is another of those with English ancestry. He used the film as the starting point for his lecture and explained how the missions had flourished for nearly 200 years, fostering amazing levels of farming and cultural achievements. Indians learned to make string and woodwind instruments, to compose music and perform in orchestras. Beautiful buildings were one of their artistic achievements. The Jesuits encouraged skills for independent living and self-government by the indigenous people, thus becoming a threat to the colonial administrators, who were

IGUAZÚ AND A JESUIT PRIEST IMPRESSED US ALL.

more interested in a source of free or cheap labour for their industries. The Indians were driven from the missions and the priests from the country. Only the ruins are there to record a period of enlightened but frustrated development.

As an academic Padre Miguel was trying hard to give an objective overview of the efforts of his predecessors in the order, and the political reasons for their eventual downfall. I was interested to note that he became so emotionally involved in telling the history of the missions that he would sometimes refer to 'us' rather than 'them'. Some of my group claimed that his talk stood out among the many lectures they had heard, and I had to agree.

When we left by plane after two wonderful days at Iguazú, I noticed that Charles was carrying Nancy's cabin bag. A nice man, I thought. We were headed for Rio de Janeiro, Brazil's best known city, but we stopped briefly at São Paulo on the way. With a population of over eighteen million, São Paulo ranks as one of the largest cities in the world, and yet it is unknown to many Australians. Landing at Rio airport it was a short journey to Copacabana, perhaps the most famous of its localities.

Copacabana boasts one of the world's best known beaches and is proud of the numerous hotels facing it. We stayed in the Hotel Copacabana Palace, a wonderful 1920s building with great character and very well maintained. Pictures of royalty from many countries, world leaders and great film stars lined one of the walls, indicating that they had stayed there before us. An Australian flag flew high on its mast at the front of the building. The manager explained that he had bought it just before our visit, for they had not had many Australian guests.

We were joined at dinner that night by our Australian Ambassador, Mr Charles Mott, and our Consul in Rio, Mr Peter Mason. It was a prelude to a seminar the following morning when they were joined by the former president of the Central Bank of Brazil who had been credited with planning Brazil's current economic reform. Our group included a number of business people and we were all interested in international affairs and economic development, so we found the seminar most useful. Australians know so little about Brazil, the fifth most populous country in the world and one which could be so significant to Australia in terms of world trade.

I often say that Sydney has the best harbour setting in the world. If any place could challenge that it would be Rio de Janeiro. We had a wonderful afternoon doing the tourist thing and seeing it from its many vantage points. The cable car ride to the Sugarloaf, that landmark that instantly identifies Rio, was a highlight.

Copacabana is one of the world's most famous beaches. Gently sloping clean sand with good rolling waves make it the sort of beach to relax on, with the challenge of a good body-surf as well. Swimsuits are a must on the main part of the beach, but those with beautiful bodies sport the briefest ones possible.

A walk across the road from each hotel at Copacabana brings you to an area fenced off and supervised by hotel staff and lifeguards. There are deck chairs for each hotel's guests, a plentiful supply of towels and you are carefully watched over against any dangers in the surf—or from human predators. The system works well, although it is a long way from the carefree days we spend informally on our Australian beaches.

As the sun dips behind the hotels each evening, the lifeguards pack up the chairs and other equipment and leave the beach deserted—well, nearly deserted. This was the setting that attracted Charles and Nancy to take a romantic walk along the beach in the sunset. They were not the only ones on the beach that evening, though. Two young men, jogging apparently innocently toward them, suddenly stopped, drew knives from their belts and demanded 'money, money, money'. Incidents like this, I'm afraid, are not unusual. In fact neither Charles nor Nancy had a wallet or money of any sort and after satisfying themselves of this the two scoundrels ran off.

While they were not physically harmed, Charles and Nancy were in a state of shock as they staggered into the lobby of the hotel. The manager saw their distress and ushered them into a sitting room just as Father Jim appeared on the scene. Our faithful priest, well experienced in counselling those in trauma, rose to the occasion. He sat quietly with them talking out the episode and calming their fears. An experience like this is a nasty one anywhere, but in an unfamiliar place on the other side of the world the shock is even greater. Perhaps the incident proved to be a catalyst in the growing relationship between Charles and Nancy.

Travelling is not always easy as some had just learned. I must say that I was not excited either to discover that the only practical flight between Rio and Lima, our next port of call, was a night-time one. In fact the distance between these two cities on the east and west coasts is greater than from Sydney to Perth.

We arrived in Lima, the capital of Peru, about 2.30 am. Our half-awake team struggled with the immigration cards, printed in Spanish, before we were met by a guide and taken to our coach for the ride to our hotel. Looking up from my seat to see a well-dressed young man enter our bus and walk to the back, I noticed the unmistakable bulge of a gun on his belt. An older, heavily built man climbed on board and sat in the front seat. As the bus took off I saw a police car and two police bicycles in front, and another police car and bike behind.

Peru's Ambassador in Australia had written before we left saying that he hoped we would have a good time in Peru and that we would be well looked after. This is over the top, I thought as I eyed off our bodyguards. A few months after our visit, though, there was a long and fatal siege in the Japanese embassy in Lima. In retrospect I realise that they really were giving us careful security because we travelled with a former PM.

Our few days in Lima left us with some everlasting memories. I was delighted by the Monument to Love which had been built beside the barren coast. A Spanish philosopher once noted that there are many monuments to war, but in all the world there is no monument to love—so the people of Lima built one. The centrepiece is an amusing huge Picasso-esque statue of two lovers embracing. There are plaques in many languages with quotable quotes about love. Full marks for the concept, we thought as we posed for some pics.

A delightful young guide named Alejandra showed us Lima. She told us of the time she went to the United States with her husband, who bought her an umbrella for the occasion. She had photos taken with the umbrella, but when it started to rain she had to run inside as she didn't know how an umbrella worked. Unbelievably, it never rains in Lima. The only reason it has lovely green parks and many of the houses have flower gardens is because it is located between two good rivers and they have wonderful irrigation—but it doesn't rain.

The centre of Lima has been listed as a World Heritage site. Its narrow streets contain the most splendid collection of Spanish colonial buildings in the world, and the wooden boxed balconies make it particularly fascinating. We visited a charming wooden house of this style built around a central courtyard. It has been a private residence belonging to the one family since it was constructed in the sixteenth century. The cathedral nearby, which has bamboo and adobe walls with a vaulted wooden ceiling, holds the remains of Francisco Pizarro, the *conquistador*—saint or sinner, I wondered. Certainly it's a fascinating city, and I was so glad we could visit it.

Most visitors to Lima make a point of going to the 'gold' museum, so who were we to miss out? In fact it is a museum containing much about the pre-Columbian cultures of Peru, of which the Incas are the best known. Certainly the gold and silver treasures in the museum are quite stunning, but there is so much else of value.

Our escort of bodyguards continued with us for the whole of our stay in Lima. In a traffic-congested city they proved to be a great help, simply stopping the traffic even if the red lights were against us. As well as the designated team, the local traffic police would often join in the convoy. It really was a bit much, and it did have its difficulties—at meal times we had to feed all twelve security staff in the cavalcade!

We had a change of chief of security one morning, and apparently she had not been fully briefed on her task for the day. She was a fearsome woman dressed in a navy blue suit and bright red shoes, and she walked up to John in the foyer of our hotel and addressed him in Spanish. A young man who was also a guest at the hotel offered to help with the language problem. He listened carefully to her then turned to John in surprise and said, 'You have someone in your group who is either very important or very dangerous.' When I arrived in the foyer John was busy trying to assure our new security head that EG Whitlam was not dangerous.

Our excursion that day was not one you would encounter on a normal tourist itinerary. Lima has experienced enormous population growth over a number of decades and on the outskirts of the city there are huge housing developments. We went to one of these, San Martin de Porres, where the housing developments are largely cooperative efforts by the new settlers who have come from rural areas. They build their own homes out of fairly crude concrete blocks. There is some sort of local regulation that says you don't start paying rates until your house

DOING GOOD WITH A SMILE.

is finished, which probably explains why, in the whole of this huge area, I did not see a finished house! Keeping in mind that it never rains, it may not be hard to imagine the scene that met us—miles of unbroken grey in a dusty landscape. The level of income is low, but I was impressed by the sense of pride in what they were doing and the strong sense of community spirit. Not surprisingly, the crime rate was very low.

Our interest in visiting this other side of South American life was stimulated by the fact that five Australians are working with the people of San Martin de Porres to assist in community development. We met two priests who have built recreation facilities and a chapel with funds provided by churches in Australia. It is on the side of a dirt-heaped ridge named Cornhill. Three Australian nuns help in a wide range of welfare activities, particularly involving women and children. Their acceptance into the community was shown by the warm welcome that we received from 'their' people—lots of kisses and glasses of Incacola, a bright green soft drink. I talked with one of the Peruvian women who I thought was my own age, but discovered that she was just fifty-one! I can only compliment these Australian women on their commitment to a difficult but worthwhile task. Their leader is Patricia, a comely young woman who spent three years in Chile before taking up this task in Lima. They have no car but rely on funny old buses, or they walk.

As I look back at what I have written about Lima—no rain, heavily armed guards, Spanish colonial buildings, square miles of grey housing developments—I realise that I have failed to communicate that Lima is also a city with some great boulevards, modern office buildings and beautiful houses, some at the top of the sheer cliffs where the waves of the Pacific Ocean pound at their base. As I stood on one of the lookouts on the cliffs I was reminded that there is no land mass due west across the ocean before the tip of Cape York in Australia. In fact the navigator Torres, for whom the strait above Cape York is named, sailed to the north of Australia from the port at Lima.

Lima has some interesting remains of pre-Columbian civilisations, but to see the land of the Incas it is necessary to fly to Cuzco in the Andes. It had been the capital of the Inca empire until Francisco Pizarro arrived in 1533 and proceeded to destroy this great civilisation. Most flights for the journey to Cuzco from Lima are scheduled for early morning, when the weather is usually good, so we had to start our ten-day Andean journey at seven.

Cuzco has an altitude of 3416 metres and we had to make a major adjustment to the low pressure and even lower oxygen levels. Before we left the Andes we would be at heights of more than 4000 metres. We followed the advice we were given— drink the coca tea provided, go to bed for the first few hours and eat no food until you have adjusted. That first evening I didn't feel at all well, and Gough was woozy too.

When it came time to explore our new environment I found that we were indeed in a fascinating place. The hotel was pure Spanish colonial in style and our bedroom looked out into the courtyard. I discovered that the building had been Pizarro's palace back in the sixteenth century. It was largely unchanged from that time, although I was glad they had updated the plumbing.

As we walked the streets we soon learned to identify the typical Inca structures built of enormous granite stones—cubes where each face is a metre square or more. The stones are not identical in shape but they fit together like a giant jigsaw puzzle, with no mortar used between them. Examined up close one sees that they have been carved so perfectly that it is not possible to squeeze a needle between any two of the rocks.

Among the Inca buildings are the houses, markets and churches that came following the Spanish conquest. Some of these, like the cathedral church of the Campania, are very fine indeed. For the most part the Inca and Spanish buildings, like the peoples of the same empires, have melded into a modern city and a modern people. The cruelty of the Spanish conquerors, together with the ghastly human sacrifices of the Incas, have been relegated to the past.

The present population of Cuzco, in excess of 200 000, is about the same as it was before the arrival of the Spanish.

At that time Cuzco ruled over an empire of more than thirteen million people spread across a large area of the Andes. When we realise that they had neither animals for transport nor a written language, their achievement becomes very remarkable. In the marketplace nearby, we were importuned by bauble sellers young and old. I fell for few, though I did buy a string of lapis lazuli that I still have and value and, like the rest of our group, bought alpaca sweaters, beige for me and grey for Gough.

There are only two ways of getting to Machu Picchu, the 'lost city' of the Incas. Each year many Australians take the traditional way—they walk for two or three days. The other way is by train, a method that allows a visit to be made in one full but wonderful day—and that was the way we went. Although the journey takes several hours it is through interesting and mountainous country and is punctuated by stations with hosts of descendants of the Incas peddling their colourful wares. As the elevation of Machu Picchu is several hundred metres lower than Cuzco we began to breathe more easily and that added to the sheer joy of the visit.

Pictures of Machu Picchu showing a single mountain rising behind stone ruins terraced in the foreground are readily recognisable. What is not apparent from those pictures is the extent, ruggedness and beauty of the mountain range which hid this Inca city from the Spanish intruders, and their successors, for hundreds of years. It was only in 1911 that the 'lost city' was found. By then a sense of its heritage value was realised. While a hotel and restaurants have been built outside the city, Machu Picchu remains much as it was found—which is much as it was when the Incas left. The main entrance to the site is the start

A GOOD PART OF A GOOD GROUP CONTEMPLATE A CORNER OF MACHU PICCHU.

of a pathway around the side of a hill. When the full vista of the ruined city opens up, it is magnificent.

We spent some days at the Hotel Libertador in Cuzco. The extended stay was well worthwhile. In the surrounding area are Inca fortresses, former Spanish mission buildings and local market towns set in a stark but fascinating landscape. To us the use of biblical names introduced by the Spanish is rather quaint. One morning we had a smiling Angel as the doorman of the hotel. When we returned in the evening, Jesus was there to welcome us home.

Professor Barreda Murillo came to lecture to us one evening. He had spent his entire life studying the Inca civilisation, the last thirty years at the San Antonio University in Cuzco. Naturally he was able to answer the questions that still puzzled us.

I really liked the restaurant food throughout the Andes. This is the land which gave the Irish the potato, the Scots their tatties and Germans *kartoffel*, but there are more exciting spiced dishes on the menu as well. We avoided guinea pig, but there was much fun one evening when a tourist at another table ordered one unknowingly. Dinner invariably comes garnished with music from a live pipe band playing the unique Andean music. One evening we had a rather special dinner and music at the restaurant El Truco in Cuzco. The band was playing a Latin American rhythm and the leader suggested some might like to dance. A few couples went to the dance floor, among them Laurent and Jill, that quiet couple who had joined us for the first time on this tour. Well, they overwhelmed us with their brilliant Latin American dancing—they are great company and full of fun.

To continue our journey south through the Andes required a trek of about 300 kilometres to Lake Titicaca. There is a train connecting Cuzco with Puno at the north end of the lake. It takes a very full day and has a reputation of being a particularly rough ride. We gave those in our group the option of taking the train or flying the leg on a scheduled air service. All except two opted to fly. Robin and Alison, those erudite travellers who want to know about and experience everything they possibly can, decided on the train journey, which meant a 6 am start from Cuzco. Twelve hours later they joined us in Puno. Was it worthwhile? 'Yes,' they affirmed. The flat, open, stark countryside was startling. The journey had not been easy. We could only admire their determination.

Lake Titicaca has an elevation of 3812 metres, so breathing and moving was a little harder than at Cuzco. Some members of our group were starting to show the effects of the altitude.

Clare was looking quite unwell and Nell was too sick to produce a ditty. Dr Hugh told me of his concern about their health. Particularly when the body is at rest at night, even a small movement requires extra energy, which can be debilitating. John complained that when he went to the bathroom during the night, the effort made his heart pound so much that it was difficult to get back to sleep. I pointed out that it was all right for the men—some of us had difficulty just raising ourselves from the seat!

On our journey the following morning along the western side of Lake Titicaca we had fantastic views of the lake against a backdrop of the snow covered high Andes. Thin air and a cloudless sky ensured that the lake was an emerald blue. By late morning we had crossed the border into Bolivia and were headed for lunch in a town with the familiar sounding name of Copacabana. The road was a narrow gravel one and progress was slow. We came to a culvert under repair, but the workmen had knocked off for an extended lunch. The bus tried to cross it and ended up with its front wheels suspended in the air. In our years of group travel we have had a few stranded buses, but this one seemed the most hopeless. Forty minutes of carrying rocks and packing them under the front and back wheels, a team effort by all our group, had us bumping along the road again.

After lunch beside the lake at Copacabana we went into town and discovered how the eponymous beach in Rio got its name. The Bolivian Copacabana is simply the Indian name for this locality. When the Spanish arrived they found that the locals revered a black idol, which they claimed gave them protection while sailing on the sometimes turbulent Lake

Titicaca. It was easy for the priests to replace this with a black Madonna—Our Lady of Copacabana. Some years later, when a ship was wrecked south of the port of Rio, one of the sailors convinced his colleagues to pray to Our Lady of Copacabana who, he assured them, was very efficacious in troubled waters. The sailors did land safely on the beach, uninhabited at the time, and erected a rough memorial to Copacabana—a name that was permanently adopted and became famous.

There is a little twist to the story about the famous black Madonna at Copacabana in Bolivia. It is believed that safety on Lake Titicaca is only ensured when the Madonna is actually facing the lake. The statue was erected behind the altar of the great white and blue church, which we visited. The church fronts the lake, so the Madonna would normally have her back to the water. The problem was solved by mounting the statue on a rotating platform, these days operated by electricity. Six days a week she looks out over the lake, but on Sundays she is turned to face the congregation. Few care to sail on Sundays.

Our journey continued by boat across the lake to the settlement of Huatajata. The resort hotel there has been built to encourage an understanding of Aymara Indian traditions. There are men who build reed boats, including one man who went to Egypt to help Thor Heydal build the reed boat for a successful crossing of the Atlantic, giving credence to the possibility that there may have been communication in this way between ancient cultures. At night we observed the stars blazing through a thin crisp sky, and learned something of Aymara cosmology.

Some of us thought it was a bit of fun to visit Lorenzo, the resort's soothsayer or witch doctor. His techniques had been handed down for centuries, or so he said, and we watched him do his stuff cooking up coca leaves before several of the group posed rather trivial questions about the future. A more serious Charles asked our seer, 'Will I marry again?' There was an equally serious reply in the affirmative.

Clare's condition had deteriorated and it was now a matter for concern. Hugh listened to her noisy breathing, and to her heart, and increased the treatment of antibiotics. We arranged for her to be in a room near Anne and John and they checked her regularly during the night.

Early in the morning John went to see how Clare was, and when he could not rouse her or feel her pulse he called for Hugh, who was there in seconds. Grabbing the oxygen cylinder he started his desperate efforts to resuscitate her. There was relief all round as breathing, though troubled, could be heard again. 'We must get her to a hospital urgently,' Hugh announced. We were fifty kilometres from La Paz, capital of Bolivia. John phoned a contact he had in La Paz, who recommended that we take our patient to the hospital in the city operated by a German organisation with German doctors. The manager of the hotel was roused and he thought it was better that he drive Clare himself rather than wait for an ambulance. Two hours later we were relieved to hear that Dr Hugh and Clare had arrived safely at the German hospital, where Clare was now receiving specialist treatment.

During the afternoon the rest of our group travelled into La Paz, a Spanish name meaning 'peace'. From a vantage point we could see the city stretching before us, many of its houses clinging to steep hillsides around the narrow valley that forms the centre of the city. It is the highest capital city in the world and our Hotel Presidente was the tallest building in the city—

right opposite the main market square and the historic church and monastery dedicated to St Francis of Assisi.

While La Paz may have similarities to other capital cities in South America or indeed the world—including a suitably impressive parliament, president's palace, cathedral, attractive city square—out of town is totally different. Some valleys right beside the city have the appearance of moonscapes. They are devoid of vegetation and quite unlike any other place I have seen. We passed a golf course where some grass had been induced to grow on a more level piece of land. In a city that is noted for records associated with altitude, it was not surprising to learn that not only is it the highest golf course in the world but someone there had created a record for the longest drive with a golf ball!

A trip seventy-two kilometres out of La Paz took us one day to Tiwanaku, the capital of a pre-Inca civilisation near Lake Titicaca. We had become familiar with the great carved stones of the Incas, but here a much older civilisation had already mastered the skill of carving and placing huge stones. Archaeologists have cleared the vegetation from a large area. Former temples appear to be dedicated to the worship of the sun. We were amazed to discover that scientists now estimate that the era of the construction of this civilisation may predate the civilisations of Egypt and China.

Simón Bolívar and José de San Martin were the two great liberators of South America. Bolívar was the liberator and national hero of Colombia, Venezuela, Ecuador, Peru and Bolivia. Upper Peru was named Bolivia after the liberator and was recognised in 1825 as a separate country. For the next 150 years the government changed very frequently, usually by revolution. The last military coup took place some twenty years before our visit, and compulsory voting seems to have provided the key to greater political stability and progress.

To understand more about the current situation in Bolivia we arranged for the director of the government agency concerned with coordinating social development to talk to us about the plans under way to increase educational opportunities and health. We were encouraged to hear about action already in progress in a country noted for its lack of development.

On our last day we were to have Gonzalo Montenegro as our speaker. Mr Montenegro had been Ambassador to Australia and concurrently to a number of Pacific and South East Asian countries. He was now a senior member of the parliament with particular interests in economic development. On the morning of his talk we saw crowds of people gathering in the market square and around the Church of St Francis. We learned that farmers and rural workers were blockading the city in protest over prices for their produce, and that they planned to march on parliament at 5 pm—the time scheduled for Mr Montenegro to speak to us. We were more concerned when truckloads of armed troops appeared in the city to guard the parliament. We went to the front door of our hotel to discover that we were sealed in by soldiers standing shoulder to shoulder right around the building.

Unsure whether our speaker would be able to get to the hotel, we gathered in the conference room on the fourteenth floor. From the windows we could see the crowds starting to move towards the parliament. They had to pass our hotel on the way. Right on time a smiling Gonzalo Montenegro walked into the conference room. He explained that he knew his way from the parliament through narrow back lanes and had entered a side door of the hotel without incident.

His talk was an inspiration. He told of earlier days when Bolivia's economy was built on silver mining and described the dreadful conditions under which the miners lived, worked and died. Well-equipped with maps and charts he showed where there were huge reserves of natural gas in that part of the Amazon basin which belongs to Bolivia, and the well-advanced construction of a gas pipeline to Brazil—it has since been completed. He was frank about the potentials of development, as well as the social and political problems that come with it.

As he was speaking we could hear the noise of the throngs outside the hotel, despite the fact that it was a closed, air-conditioned building and we were so high up in it. Several dull thuds came in quick succession. 'That's tear gas,' Montenegro commented without pausing in his talk. We soon knew ourselves what it was for our own eyes were reddening, then some began to cough and splutter as the gas found its way up the lift well and through the air-conditioning.

A little later there were several very loud bangs. 'That's gelignite!' This time he did pause to relate something of his days as an activist in great marches. 'I loved the way the silver miners would walk along smoking cigars and carrying sticks of gelignite. They would light them with their cigars and throw them at exactly the right moment for them to explode high in the air.' We realised that this was happening now right beside us.

As darkness came the tumult and the shouting died. We had felt secure in the hotel and appreciated that we had had a first-hand experience of another aspect of South American life. We had dinner in the restaurant on the top floor. The 360 degree view was of millions of twinkling lights, some bright and star-like on the hills enclosing and reaching far higher than us. Many of them in the business district immediately below us were coloured. Above the electric lights the real stars burned brightly through the thin air of the sky. We were certainly in a different world.

Clare was missing from our farewell dinner. In the hospital the doctors had diagnosed pneumonia, which they felt had probably been with her in a mild form before the trip, but had flared up in the high altitude of the Andes. She was improving and the hospital and airline agreed that she could fly home to Australia in the company of Dr Hugh, provided oxygen and other medical necessities were on hand.

After ten days in the Andes we had certainly adjusted to the altitude, but still had difficulty breathing and exerting ourselves. We boarded the plane at La Paz and commenced the extra long charge down the runway—one of the requirements when taking off in the low pressure of the world's highest commercial airport. As the plane pressurised we could breathe more easily and a sense of relief came over the group. As we landed at sea level in Buenos Aires, the relief was more a euphoria.

Marina Begg met us in Buenos Aires during our brief stop there. She was anxious to hear of our experiences on the journey as she had played such a vital part in the planning and arrangements for us. She was pleased that we had enjoyed the whole experience and learned a lot, and that the six speakers had been so helpful. She was fascinated by our stories of the hold-up at Copacabana, the security convoy in Lima, the medical crisis by Lake Titicaca and the riots in La Paz. Our study tour had been one with a difference.

Marina waved us goodbye as we left for the flight back to Australia. She wrote later: 'When I saw you off on your way home, I had a feeling as if I had just come to the end of a really good book.'

9

MY WORLD IN REVIEW

THAT IS MY OTHER WORLD. My own real world is, of course, Australia. No matter where I travel, how impressed I am or how much I love places and people in my other world, the best part of being away is coming home.

Sydney is the city of my birth and I have lived there most of my life, so naturally I identify with it most strongly. I love the harbour shores with the good, the bad and even the ugly, from the stark symmetry of the bridge to the graceful curves of the Opera House. The golden sandstone buildings of nineteenth-century Sydney—the Town Hall, the cathedrals, Sydney University, the Lands Department, the Art Gallery—give us some of the most attractive cityscapes in the world. The mixture of residential styles around the harbour provides an environment that is second to none. Our sprawling suburbs now have facilities which few large cities can match.

Biased as I may be towards Sydney, it is a pleasure to visit our other states—their capitals, provincial cities and rural areas. In Melbourne I love to take the tram out to St Kilda or around the city centre on the freebie, not to mention the city's art centre.

South Australia has the luxuriant wineries so accessible to Adelaide with its parks and gardens. Perth is always enjoyable, but I wish it was closer to the eastern states so that we could visit more easily. What a treat our Apple Isle is where, these days, its cheeses add to the good things produced there. Queensland is so laid-back that Brisbane always produces a surprise.

Canberra is a pleasant city to live in and I still enjoy visiting. Young families appreciate the simplicity of life, the convenience of excellent schools, and the good sporting and cultural facilities. It has health services of a very high standard. Similar provisions for a good quality of life are often now to be found in the larger regional centres across Australia.

For me, one of the most interesting aspects of travel has always been attending musical and other performances in theatres around the world. Certainly the great theatres of Europe, like the Bolshoi in Moscow, the Semperoper in Dresden, the Paris opera or the Vienna Staatsoper, are impressive for their appearance and stirring because of their traditions. On the other hand we have concerts, opera and ballet in Australia which are among the best in the world. And for the most part we do not have to pay as much as in most European countries to experience these top class performances. The same now applies to Australian restaurants and Australian wines—we stand high among the world's best. We have a unique and scenic countryside of which we can be so proud—I just wish that we were in a fly-free zone.

People often ask me which is my favourite 'other' country and a frequent answer is, 'The one I was in last.' It is good to become involved in any country that you visit. Of course there are things that make each one unique and desirable.

My favourite city? An even harder question to answer. I know that I would be delighted to spend next weekend in Paris, Prague, Vienna, Venice and always London. But then I would be equally content to choose a quiet weekend in Provence, by Windermere, on Mt Rigi, beside the sea in Positano or in a garden resort in northern Thailand.

People sometimes ask me for advice about places to visit. It's a question that raises important issues in relation to responsibility and the value of travel. Many people travel simply for a holiday—to stretch out on the beach of some Asian resort, or to put their feet up in some place where the food, drink and service is good. Most people, however, want to learn and experience new things. I think of them as travellers rather than tourists.

It is important that we get to know our neighbours, and Australians with the means should try to visit Indonesia, New Zealand or one of the Pacific islands. Travel is so valuable in extending international understanding and world peace. Then I suggest that people should travel to places that are most significant to *them*. As a nation founded on migrants, many of us use travel to understand more about our origins. I sometimes think that our best travellers are those who are actually pilgrims—not in the religious sense, but having a real purpose in visiting places of personal significance, perhaps places that are important in their profession, or are known to them through history, music or literature.

There is a great satisfaction in seeing places that we have only been able to imagine, though they may be important in our lives. I remember the thrill of seeing the Parthenon and the Taj Mahal for the first time. I remember my daughter's excitement at seeing Piccadilly and Leicester Square and realising that they were not just names in a board game, but real places.

Centuries ago tourist travel was always in the form of pilgrimages to holy shrines. It provided a purpose and structure for those with sufficient willpower and means to travel. In later centuries there was the 'grand tour', considered necessary to complete an education based on a study of the classics. It also had merit in providing the basis of a plan for travel. There seems to be lots of evidence that whether people were on a pilgrimage or a grand tour they had plenty of enjoyment as they travelled. Modern travellers may like to consider building an itinerary around UNESCO World Heritage sites, as we have on occasions. These have been identified either because of their historical and cultural significance or because they have a unique natural environment. On mainland Britain, for instance, the World Heritage sites include Westminster, the Tower of London, Canterbury Cathedral, Blenheim Palace, Stonehenge, Bath, Ironbridge Gorge, the castles of northern Wales, Fountains Abbey in Yorkshire, Durham Castle and Cathedral, Hadrian's Wall, and Edinburgh. An itinerary planned to include those sites would give anyone a really good tour of Britain. UNESCO has now identified World Heritage sites in most countries and details can readily be found on the Internet.

I have concerns about the future of travel to some of the places that have been popular destinations around the world. These days, particularly in the height of the tourist season, it is necessary to queue for hours to get into places like the Uffizi Gallery in Florence, the Sistine Chapel in Rome or the Louvre in Paris. The Palace of Versailles copes at present with the thousands who visit each day, but it may be necessary to walk shoulder to shoulder in a human mass through the Hall of Mirrors. As air travel continues to become comparatively cheaper and more people are able to travel, the crowds will continue to increase. Similarly, I have concerns about the effect of tourism on some of the more delicate natural and cultural environments of the world. Environmentalists have expressed fears about the effects of increased tourism on Fraser Island's ecosystem, while the social structures in places like Bali and some of the Pacific islands have been done irreparable harm by tourism.

We have encouraged our groups to eat the regional foods in countries that we visit as one of the best ways of experiencing a country is to eat the local food in the local way and at the local time. This may mean having dinner at 10 pm in the Hispanic countries, or eating the main meal in the middle of the day in Russia. Some people expect their own ways of eating and living to be provided for them in another country. Why bother to leave home if you want to take your kitchen and dining room with you?

We need to respect the local customs and religious beliefs of the countries we are visiting. Being conscious of the dress standards and expectations of our hosts is also important. I have joined the locals in services and ceremonies of many different religions around the world, though of course one has to be sensitive about the extent to which they want you to join in. The Loi Kratong festival in Thailand, where we were part of the celebrations, was a particularly rich experience.

It's always a good idea to attempt a few words in the language of a new country. I find that it's not very difficult to learn a few courtesy words like 'please' and 'thank you' in any language. Together with a smile, these words can break down a lot of barriers. We can probably manage more words and phrases in local languages when we visit Western Europe. 'Have a go,' I encourage people on my tours. 'Try to read the notices and try to speak a little.' Even when in Russia, most of the letters in the Cyrillic alphabet can be learned in an hour or two, and this makes it possible to read many signs if the words are similar to English.

Some people have questioned my enthusiasm for visiting Britain and enjoying something of the pomp and ceremony. To them I must say that you don't have to be a royalist to be a loyalist—I look forward to my country's true independence when it becomes a republic, but I respect the status quo and enjoy it to the hilt. I'm sure that Elgar will always be one of my favourite composers, just as I enjoy the national composers of many other countries. A recent three-day celebration in London for the centenary of the Australian Federation Bill passing through the British Parliament showed the world that Britain and our Queen are very aware of the state of our nationhood. Her Majesty and her successor, the Prince of Wales, took part in our ceremonies, and former Australian prime ministers were entertained right royally.

As an octogenarian, I know that some of my contemporaries believe that I am probably too old to travel. Age has very little to do with it, and in any case age is always a poor indicator of performance. Health and mobility, however, are important factors. What do you do with the older traveller? You respect her (it is more likely to be *her* than *him*). I remember an eighty-two year old on one of our first tours being the most spritely of the group and moving faster than anyone up and down hills, and in and out of castles. That category now includes me, but I'm getting stronger all the time—so much so that I am seriously thinking of going back to competition golf—or perhaps, more realistically, regular golf. When I think of group travel it's come one, come all, as far as I'm concerned.

Those contemplating overseas travel are usually faced with the question: 'Can I travel independently? Could I bear being on a group tour?' I've travelled both ways and appreciate the advantages of both. One would have to be rather brave or foolish to travel independently through some countries in, say, Central or Eastern Europe. Not only can there be problems in relation to language and personal security, but people alone or in pairs are often given little consideration when it comes to accommodation, meals and inspection of sites. You don't have the back-up that group travel provides if you have an accident or illness. Jim and Elsie, who travelled to Germany with us, had been there twelve months earlier as independent travellers. They told me 'the two visits highlighted the advantages and disadvantages of organised tours and independent travel. The latter allows personal choice of itinerary and time spent in museums, galleries etc., while the former packages the "targets" more efficiently and removes all strain of suitcases, meals and transport. Both worked well for us.'

In Western Europe travelling alone is quite safe and easy. In Britain and Ireland we speak similar languages, and drive on the same side of the road, so many Australians opt for renting a car and taking advantage of the great range of accommodation available. I, too, have done this in my younger days and have enjoyed it immensely, but the only way to save money as an independent traveller is to lower the quality of the accommodation and food. On a number of ISP tours we have kept a check of the price of the accommodation, meals and entry fees that one would have had to pay as an independent traveller. In every case it proves to be more expensive than the price we were able to charge for a group tour. Such are the benefits of group rates.

An enormous amount of planning precedes a successful group tour. Many independent travellers have found that, had they been a day earlier or later, they would have caught a particular performance or been able to visit a special art museum. It requires a lot of work by an individual traveller to match a good group tour organiser in getting the most out of the time available. The services of good local guides and a tour leader add to the richness of the travel experience. I think I've mentioned a number of situations in this book which could never have been experienced by a person travelling independently. Travelling in the company of people with common interests can also be very stimulating.

The Whitlams, with John and Anne, seemed to have constituted a rather special foursome to lead tours throughout the nineties. We were certainly encouraged to continue by the feedback from travellers on our tours. 'In some way the Whitlams pulled the group together; gave it point and direction. That inimitable Whitlam wit, wisdom and presence says it all,' one of our travellers reported. Maybe that's a bit over the top, but I was pleased to read: 'Margaret's friendly manner and sense of humour put everyone at ease.' About Anne and John someone wrote: 'They are excellent organisers and wonderfully interesting people as well'. Another said of the way they managed yet another tour: 'The Anne and John magic goes from strength to strength'—and indeed it did. In the latter years the Whitlam tours were not advertised. On the suggestion that we were planning another journey or adventure, all the places would be filled by people who had travelled with us before—even before the actual itinerary was announced. Perhaps that was the greatest compliment of all.

I have been able to tell you about a few of those who travelled with us, and of some of the people who helped us along the way. In fact there were hundreds of different people who travelled with me. Then there were dozens of local guides, coach drivers, hosts at hotels and others who made those tours into memorable experiences. Everyone I have described in this book is a real person and in almost every case I have used their real names. Every story is true.

Each traveller and each guide was unique and as I look down a list of their names I remember each one and say to myself, 'She was the one who nearly walked in front of the bus in Prague', or 'He was the one who always had a bag of peppermints to sustain us on late arrivals'. I have kept up with many of them and am able to tell you a little more.

Mary still teaches history and English. She describes the Parthenon in a way only possible by one who has ascended the heights of the Acropolis. Her lessons about Wordsworth have a special inspiration. I suspect that she tells her pupils that the Sheriff of Nottingham, who harassed Robin Hood, was probably a really nice man—just misunderstood.

Alison and Robin have chalked up a record twelve ISP tours. Their general knowledge has been a great help as we travelled. They continue to get the very most from the tours, always travelling a little further than the others. On a recent ISP tour to Bhutan, Robin climbed to the Tigers Nest Monastery, an achievement far beyond the stamina and willpower of many much younger people. Alison, however, has not attempted to take any more unscheduled flights in China.

Margaret from Ballarat always has an aria at the ready in case she happens across an amphitheatre requiring a test of its acoustics.

Betty is no longer with us. I like to think of the wonderful smile she may have had as she looked past St Peter and exclaimed, 'Magnifique!'

Hetty died soon after her visit to Berlin. I am so glad that we were able to stand with her in her personal pilgrimage to the place of her childhood.

Clare recovered completely from her ordeal in the Andes and still travels the world with ISP.

The good Dr Hugh continues to help those who need his skills, though that dawn in the Andes when he clutched Clare back from a near death experience was among his finest hours.

The oracle beside Lake Titicaca who told Charles that he would marry again proved to be correct. Charles married Nancy the following year. The 'bairn from Nairn' proudly wore the tartan kilt of the Robertson clan at the wedding. They are well on the way to living happily ever after.

Father Jim has sworn off vodka, but still counsels those in need and always has a suitable prayer to conclude every event.

Things didn't work out for our wonderful Russian guide, Mariana. The marriage proposed to her by our Australian man did not eventuate. But then in Russia things often work out sadly.

Horst continues to guide groups through Salzburg with a dry wit and a sharp tongue for anyone not paying attention.

Richard drives his big white coach through France, with a folding table in the baggage compartment in case any of those on board have the strange Australian idea of wanting a picnic by the roadside. Richard and Silvie have at last 'made a baby'—they call him Nicholas.

Mariana, Horst and Richard, together with Helga, Jane and Annop, are waiting in my other world to welcome travellers from Australia.

International Study Programs still conducts great tours, but without the Whitlams. Barry Jones, Ian and Rosemary Sinclair, Huw Evans and Peter Egan are among the tour leaders. There are new directors of the company.

John and Anne now have a conference centre just beyond the Blue Mountains. They named it Rydal Mount after one of my favourite places in my other world. They helped me write this book.

I'm going to miss that blue and white sign on the coach reading 'International Study Programs, Australia'. I loved those years of planning and leading tours. I regard them as some of the happiest of my life.

THE WHITLAM TOURS

BETWEEN 1991 AND 1999 there were eighteen tours led by Margaret and Gough Whitlam. John Wellings and Anne Krone, together or separately, were the managers of all except one of those tours.

The tours ran for a total of 389 days and involved 556 participants—not 556 different people, for some took part in several tours. The average length of each tour was twenty-one days and the average number of participants on each tour was thirty.

The tours included visits to twenty-four different countries, of which eighteen are mentioned in *My Other World*.

Here are the names of the tours, when they were held and where they went:

A Cultural Tour to Europe with Margaret Whitlam
September 1991: France, Switzerland, Italy, Austria, Czechoslovakia, Germany.

A Study Program in Eastern Europe with Gough and Margaret Whitlam
May 1992: Austria, Czechoslovakia, Germany, Russia.

A Cultural Tour to Europe with Margaret Whitlam
September 1992: France, Switzerland, Italy, Austria, Czechoslovakia.

Thailand—A Northern Experience with Gough and Margaret Whitlam
November 1992: Thailand.

A Study Program in China with Gough and Margaret Whitlam
May 1993: China, Hong Kong.

A Literary Tour of England with Margaret Whitlam
September 1993: England. Gough came on this one too.

The Great Russian Journey with Gough and Margaret Whitlam
June 1994: Japan, Russia.

Mostly Music with Margaret Whitlam
September 1994: Switzerland, Italy, Austria.

The Heart of France—A Journey with Margaret Whitlam
April/May 1995: France.

Mostly Music with Margaret Whitlam
September 1995: Switzerland, Italy, Austria. John and Robyn Rooth were the managers on this tour.

An Italian Interlude with Margaret Whitlam
May 1996: Italy. Gough came on this one too.

A Journey through South America with Gough and Margaret Whitlam
September 1996: Argentina, Brazil, Peru, Bolivia.

A Journey in Spain and Portugal with Gough and Margaret Whitlam
May 1997: Spain, Portugal.

A Cultural Tour of Germany with Gough and Margaret Whitlam
September 1997: Germany.

Greece and Turkey with Gough and Margaret Whitlam
May 1998: Greece, Turkey.

Impressions of France with Margaret Whitlam—The Artists' Lives and their Works
May/June 1998: France.

Great Experiences of Britain with Margaret Whitlam
September 1998: England, Wales, Scotland. Unfortunately Margaret was unable to participate due to an accident.

A Journey through Eastern Europe with Gough and Margaret Whitlam
September 1999: Ukraine, Romania, Hungary.

In addition to the eighteen Whitlam Tours, Margaret was involved in the planning of a further sixty-nine International Study Program tours during the 1990s. Huw Evans, best remembered as the host of *Mastermind*, led seven garden tours, gardens being his first love. Peter Egan, former ABC music presenter, led twelve music tours. Anne Krone and John Wellings led fourteen cultural tours. Other leaders and managers included Sir Neil Curry, Jane Glaser, Bill Grant, Maureen Hickson, Annette James, Patti Johnson, Barry Jones,

Mariana Kiseleva, John Lombard, Clem MacMahon, Val Street, Graham Swain, Michelle Underwood and Margaret Weekes. In total the ISP tours in that decade had 2139 participants and spent 1661 days travelling in thirty-three different countries.

Compiled by International Study Programs

We are scarcely four centuries distant from the
emancipation from slavery of a third of our species.
We are, in fact, the first animal class, the first class
which as a class can free itself from bondage to other
creatures.